COLLECTED
POEMS
Volume III

COLLECTED
POEMS
Volume III

RALPH GUSTAFSON

For Kristi
warmest wishes and friendship
Betty
In memory of Ralph.

October 17 - 1998
Nanaimo B.C.
Inauguration of Ralph Gustafson Chairs in Poetry
Malaspina University College

1994
Sono Nis Press
VICTORIA, BRITISH COLUMBIA

Canadian Cataloguing in Publication Data

Gustafson, Ralph, 1909-
 Collected poems

  ISBN 0-919203-77-9 (Vol. 1)
  ISBN 0-919203-79-5 (Vol. 2)
  ISBN 1-55039-052-X (Vol. 3)

  I. Title.
  PS8513.U7A17.1987   C811'.54   C87-091342-5
  PR9199.3.G87A17 1987

Publication financially assisted by the
Canada Council Block Grant Program

Published by
SONO NIS PRESS
1745 Blanshard Street
Victoria, British Columbia V8W 2J8

Designed and printed in Canada by
MORRISS PRINTING COMPANY LTD.
Victoria, British Columbia

For Betty

A Word About The Text

The best takes time: never more than in such a living art as poetry.

The original texts of the books presented here have occasionally been revised; the nature of poetry itself, whatever the immediate content, demands satisfaction and I have taken direction of the time I have had.

R.G.

North Hatley
1994

Contents

At the Twenty-First Century

A Window Lighted

1987
WINTER PROPHECIES

That region where the air is music.
— EMERSON

Poems for the Times

Let Us Be Tender about the Earth

Let us be tender about the earth.
From the moon: a rounded place and loved
Of blue-spun cloud and watery sphere
Imposed on the glory of scattered stars,
Leaned on the constancy of heaven.
One balance over and we are done.

Dunes slant against the sea,
Shells subside and the miles of sand
Glistened under the moon, ebb.
A man walks wobbling barefoot.
On Nubble Head the light swings round,
Waves continual search the rock.

Let us look to the affirmative earth.
Sown in spring, where the summer
Was, the marks of harvest lead
To the edge of willow-cuts and the useless
Wall of hand-piled stone,
Stop where the combine turned.

I remember the difficulty Lamarche had—
The farm at the turn of the Sherbrooke Road—
The chickens ate their own eggs,
Feeding them broken crockery no good:
The thing was to place a delivery chute
Under the hens to roost on.

A crucifixion some look to;
Others, the great stone at Mecca
Millions walk round; the prayer-wheel
Turning in the mountain wind . . . The corner
Of my house needs fixing, the wood
Fragile where the rain came in . . .

Such is the World's Outrageous Position

Such is the world's outrageous position,
Dying without reason,
We suffer gods,

A bone through our nose, pounding earth
In time to the primitive moon,
Drum up faith,

Construct perspiring heaven, announce
To the disregarding dark,
Habitation—

The jungle alive with frightened birds.
Nothing for it, our flawed
Investiture nightly

Furnished with stars, we die in ourselves
The same, the lack of knowing
Universal.

That Sunday, not believing, All-over
Beneficence incredible—
You remember?

The Easter sun out, clerical,
The architecture pleasing,
Two cushions

Available, the antependium gold
(Death now conquered)—
What's more,

The prayer-book's prose unbeatable—kneeling
Together, murdered King Richard
Holding hands

With his Anne in their tombs nearby, we laid up
Psalms *post mortem*
Just in case?

The Abbey that day was crowded. Half
False, half true,
What shall we say?

That heaven works? Given love
And Death, oblivion too
Damnable to think of,

Foliage everywhere monstrous with life,
That man with his hairy sex
Is the noble splendour?

Postscript

And so to the great theme: God and sex,
Both inextricably at one
And one denied the other,

Cradles and kingdoms crumble to ensure the friction—
The little ones beloved at last
In necessary distant heaven.

Acceptable, acceptable. OK,
No more objection, just that the union
Is inscrutable, but love

In it, as long as love is in there somewhere,
Nothing if not that, making
Both justifiable . . .

Underwater Scene

Teeming with life and all of it
Predatory, most of it useless.
The snout nubbling entrails left over
By satiation.

　　　　Inordinate context!—
Meat in the high grass, the kill
At dusk, man's wanting:
A thumb's difference.

　　　　Diving
For abalone, Rehm saw
Something shaking his friend Omar
Violently.

The Question of Priority for the Moment

From useful matters I withdraw.
I have doubtful heaven and ambiguous God
To settle accounts with, exquisite questions
About the end of the universe, decisions
Whether the stars are going anywhere
And who cares. Rather than beautiful
Turbines and exertions of power, how
Many poems the world will read
And whether lasting music exists
And why not, concern me, whether
Irony is safer than religion.

At bottom, whether the poems required
Are preferable to travelling to Venice.

Final Disquisition on the Giant Tube-Worm

On the ocean floor, topped with blood-red plumes,
The giant tube-worm feeds. It feeds on water
Laden with hot sulphur. Crabs graze
The plumes. I suppose He created the tube-worm.
I doubt it. It has no free-will, it baffles
Evolution, it lacks martyrdom, it doesn't
Need light. It is undue.

There
It ingests. Without plot of propagation.

Ions One-Thousandth the width of a Pinhead

Halley's comet in the celestial heavens
Was there even as it got embroidered
In the Bayeux tapestry when Harold
Got an arrow in the eye at Hastings
Letting Normandy into England,
Even as Liszt blazed into Raiding
And set the listening world agog,
As it hovered over Jesus
Painted by Giotto in His beastly
Manger.

    How many prophecies blasted
Across the waiting stars, some
Lies, some otherwise.

    I sit and listen. Scientists probe
How many ions make its tail
Ten million astronomical
Units outward, time and days
Enough for the answer, winter's solstice
Accounted for when the night gets
Shorter and the crocus begin to stir.
My heart in its casing counts . . .

Flowers for Hiroshima

A scorched watch timed the blast
At 8:16. 8:16
Is a little early for me but gardens
Wait even as violence,
Both according to the intensity
Of how life is loved, not too long
A wait but sufficient.

               My wife cultivates
Easter where the crowded lilies are.
We are our own crucifixion.

                       Alas
That people die.

August 5, 1985

Beethoven as an Example of the Unconditional

The absolutes are out of favour:
Beethoven who heard less and less
Though his successive trumpets grew
In size, kazoo to bamboozle,
Heard heaven, the questions asked him
Written down, the notebooks blank
Of answers whose music is the answer.
Plug. Plug. Rock against Easter
Gone, guarded by angels, so
It's said, privation out of favour.
He knew what is said.

Sun on the water

We could use transcendence,
That unheard-of greatness: standing
On Everest because it is there—
That urgence: pain
Ignored, borne with,
The possibility later thought of,
Displaced for love—that quality
Of surpassing—
The resplendent choice
That stands for the extremest soul
Recognized: the dipping in
Of the hand in praise, the greatness
Known at that blanket-plucking
Time of dying—
The anger that makes right;
What was, small.

Late May

Magnolia blossoms showed beyond
The edge of the verandah, four of them,
The evergreen hedge back of them—
Petals white and suffused pink
About to fall so well open
Were they, the awkward sun made use of,
Too far north. The wheelbarrow
Stood empty beside the tree, the shovel
Fallen. It did not matter much.
The usual hummingbird was returned
To the lilac though it was not out,
Just the leaves.

      A casual moment,
Nothing much new, what you expect
At the change of the year. I went downtown
And bought a packet of hollyhock seeds.

In the Evening

Each night in late June:
The small bird amongst the trees,
Not seen but the questioning in the far
Foliage so final the mind
Halts. An ending, the fall of song
At dusk each day always at the time
The jet comes over testing defences.
The portulaca (a flower I have learned)
Folds about then also,
The light going, the day now less,
The song too was brief, a duration
Of ten minutes perhaps? but one
You listen closely to. Down
The road two people's voices,
Too distant to make out
But they went well with the hastening melody
Of the bird and the jet referred to.

The Accident of Slight Wind and a Cobweb

Cornered sun, a slight wind and the threads
Of a cobweb suffuse running scarlet and blue
And slight green across the air. The world
Is exquisite even in its final preparations.
Consider the juxtapositions, I mean life
In its intricate astonishments: eyes, ears, sex,
Crosshatch, cross-garterings of cartilage
And conjunctions with viral accident.

                                    A man
Walks by zealously below on the street.

Saint Lawrence Roasted on one Side Asked to be Turned Over

The bluejay eats seeds swallowing
Greatly to get them down where
They won't be gotten, the roseate spoonbill
Stands in the boggy marsh for hours
On end unlike the cliffborn puffin.
Shuffle and they take off utterly.

After aeons the lizard is aware
Of itself, the tree just stands there.
Even all that so, there is more.
I have heard a child sob.
Impossible that all this should choose
Itself but it does. A creative man

Once took paper and wrote down
An abstract idea. He was so pleased
He laughed, as he went out the door
He thanked someone—effervescence,
His own brains, consequence. Other
Instances of assumption can be found—

Thumbtacks, haircuts and bedspreads,
What they stand for or hang on,
The trust of young children for instance.
Melancholy is no good:
At the instant of action everyone knows.
Dawn comes as a shock, certainty does.

Poem for the Times

Both sides won't do. We saw this
In Poland where its own tanks
Had nothing to do with true feelings in the streets
Whose want is singleness to love—individual
Windows, wives and children in them,
The streets full of festivals.
This witness was lately seen in Czechoslovakia,
In bales of tea in Boston harbour; was apparent
When Socrates drank the appointed hemlock.

The other cheek is heaven's.
Stand in Red Square
And contemplate onion-topped St. Basil's
As the tearless goosestep to the Tomb.

                        Truisms
For the statesmen. Indignation
On behalf of the single good:
Terry Fox limping across Canada.

Lest Violence be Misunderstood

Lest anyone think of love as innocence
I cite correction. Not blood
Spread on the asphalt, meshed
Where the bone is beneath the eye,
The rot in the culvert, identity
Sticking when compassion turns him over—
Red's red. Violence brought to plainness
Is nothing to what is bloodless: hurt
Done for civility, amalgamations
Of agents for the sake of God.
Odourlessness is what I mean,
Proclamations of virtue, regrets.

Of the Twelve Landscapes
— revisions

Twelve Landscapes—revisions

III   *Still the World at Dusk*

I push aside the curtain of the window
To see the glory of the world—
Not so far aside that the bare
Street bulb on the corner telephone
Pole spoils the dusk. I have watched
Beauty. The Massawippi hills
Are black against an orange sky
Going amber—the darkening north
Blue, one piercing star, mighty
Jupiter, in it northwest
Of the lower moon. The world is glory—
Without man remembered in it—
I mean, man not remembered except
His irony gone brave: Chaplin's; Falstaff
Outrageous in Eastcheap, trying on
Crowns on kitchen chairs, he
And old Shallow hearing chimes a-midnight.
Otherwise evangelists, or Khomeini
Loathing to have the riffraff in Teheran
Touch him, are what you get.

                                It's dark
The colour has gone, Jupiter still
Up, silver still—but not
Much else of note, worthy of words:
Night come, the Bologna train
About to be blown up enters
The tunnel; fundamentalists proclaim
Exclusive ownership of God.

Jagged, noble, everywhere!
In interstices of soil between
Rock, hundreds of crocuses!
Whether prophecy had
God, had doom in it,
They broke there, white,
Purple, stamens gold, petals
Six, uncounted except you bend
Down to it; colour, far, in front of you,
Out of the cold April roots
And leaves left the snow gone.
Nobility was there to see, never
Mind resurrection, good
Fridays.

        A patch of landscape,
An acre.

        You looked again
To the right, and then away
To the left, hundreds grew there!

v *The Wheatfield*

To stand alone in a field of wheat.
Sun brushes husks, the movement
Of the field hovers in the wind.

Alone, for this is the condition: to know
The maturity of all things
And have no answer, no command

Of love declaring permanence,
Of being without separation,
Its conquest of an irony. Alone

With the lost experience only.
Break off the thinking . . . The sun is hot,
The wheatfield smells of coming harvest.

Look, you have had love and though
Now alone, the birds are swift
In the grain where the ripe fulness is,

Without that memory you would not have had
Being, being here without
Submission would be a bitterness.

It is too bad, the unending sloven.
Look, this little girl and boy,
Nothing on, strut utterly
In beauty, pails in their hands hauled
Splashing to castles. The beach is crowded
With citizens, once (misfortune apart)
Of loveliness, now not once
Regretting spoilment,
What they have made it.

Where the kiteman sells his kites,
A coloured one with tails is held
At the tip by the tiny one, eager as the wind
And sand, two feet high, till the tremble
Takes it up to the sky and clouds.

Chestnuts roasted, snow falling,
To this day are loneliness.
No matter the crowd at 55th and
Sixth, the busy tapping their heels
At noon on the balustrade of the fountain,
The wind cold from the west, from the Hudson,
The charcoal brazier making bravely
Warm the southwest corner of the street,
No matter possessing love, chestnuts
In a paper bag, hard coals,
Pink steam at the corner of the city,
              a loneliness inextricable
Is in the awareness of heart that all
This glory is gone. Is it not so—
That what you love is its moment gone?
How could it be otherwise, this ambiguous
World: November, the pavement, Luigi
Old, his chestnuts eight for a dollar,
The snow falling, the street forever—
No escaping that wind from the Hudson?

Winter Prophecies

The Red Marker

That lift of dust
In the turn of the rising wind
And that which belongs to dust.

I knew the taking years ago
And still there are cities, music
I do not know.

Yesterday I put the red marker
Where I wanted the white birch planted,
Not thinking.

Not All the Highest Metaphors of Music

The irony that answers suffering and on the other hand
Saint Simeon successfully sitting his lifetime pillar.
Folks all over the region come to see
How he manages his evacuations and legs
But his boredom with prayers eventually.
They found out about the droppings if not
The prayers Dorian felt tomorrow cannot come up
Too soon to watch with her the lucky sun.

    Not all the highest metaphors
    Of music are a grace, not so.

Both were young though.

Winter Prophecies

Beyond all wisdom is the lonely heart.
Beware of love. It calls up winter prophecies.

The firewood is piled, the chimney solid . . .
And the hours are counted that leave

Belief of her astonished still.
Time is a harsh consultant. I warn

You. Without that love there is no hour.
With love are winter prophecies.

"Death Is not Lived Through"

The omission is the worst. No matter
The offering now, the moment
Is too little for what was forgotten,

The response asked for not given,
The context too trivial for regret
But asked for, made majesties by death.

Variations on a Theme of Indian Summer

1

The air was full of leaves,
Wayward, but over, over.
I had known this,
Four weeks ago the ground was covered,
I had raked the leaves from the lawn into bags.
But this was different.
The falling leaves so many
There was ending, the meaning
As in a music, ending come to,
The music wanted.
This was prophecy, assignable,
Most of all to him who loves.
Indifference, indifference
Is best, the beauty only what is
And not employed, a season.
Now through the air even
In the sun the leaves falling
Invest the heart.
It is too
Bad, this falling.

2

I retreat, I think to go indoors,
The air turns over with leaves,
The shadows catch my vision sidelong,
They are audible that should be noiseless and so
Meaningless. I am bombarded by heaven,
Succession asks that I get out of it,
There is no wind, certainly not
Since the day before yesterday has there been rain,
The air stirs only, if that,
But the glory of the tree comes down.
It is ludicrous what is happening, common,
But demanding attention. From one point
Of view it is beautiful—the sun out
On the great tree, the world turned bronze
From too much green too overstated.
But that is strategy. The aggression glances
My cheek, the top of my head, sticks
In the wool of my sweater next to the skin
Of the back of my neck. The falling is successful.

3

All is disorder. The wind sweeps
These tall elm trees
On their roots and there is turmoil—
To give, to give so there is correction.
Disorder is a taking. The heart keeps
(Grief among other things) but there is
A taking. O that the world
Should gather its grief so that there is
Order.

I listen to the tensile strength,
The great elm, as the wind
Sweeps its greatness.

Winter Arrival

The five crows sit there
Waiting for winter, ruffle, caw
And mock the fences. All's stupid.
Summer was amended long ago,
The fields ready, little of colour,
The fir, green, the same in December,
No help, four o'clock dark,
The hills dark against the sky,
Too poor to put up against
The scheme of things, the prophecy
Impairment in the world. We
Could do without five crows
Crookedly crowing on a fence
As cold progression comes. The racket
Is arrogance, the twelfth time
Snow came was acceptance.

The Road Tenders

The hedge-rows drop their snows,
Bare earth shows through at the roots,
Side-drifts thaw. Whenever the wind
Comes from the valley and in March the rain
Is a chilling rain, the harsh water
Floods down the hill over the roadway,
The buried pipe that should carry it
Broken where no one of the road
Tenders listening can find out.

Two Meditations

1   Meditation, It Being Warm

I left the door open and with the larger
Pair of scissors cut off the browned
Furlings of petunia blossoms that were in
The window-boxes so that the buds
Have lease and the day coming have
Happenings of pinwheels and gambling
Florescences. The day had been clouded,
Then from under, the sun flung
Its metaphor—meaning nothing
Ultimately, the sun would continue to shine.
But here anyway was sun,
Enough to put meditation
Out of kilter, so to speak.

No getting around it. Suspend
Pruning, sit in an easy chair
Down the pathway somewhere.

2 *Meditation, Turned Inward on the Self*

What a part of sadness, those poems—
Héloïse taking off her pale blue dress,
The moon with "her beauty stowed still,"
That "lighted window" at dusk in Sweden,
Gold on the snow.
Sixty years of poems—
And the child with a kite.

I walk alongside the split-cedar fence.
Queen-Anne's-lace is out and the mustard flower.
All that is needed:
That writing at a bedroom window,
The street below,
The nightjars swift in the air above the maple tree
In descents of flight.

The Spring in the Woods above the Lake

A consternation of cloud
white and high

looked up at
the mind is made
stubborn.

How the water-spring came cold
when the leaves were moved
in the hollow in the woods!

Only the Seasons

Only the seasons matter.
Snow on apple-blossom,
Summer come, skies
With broken cloud and rains,
Winter with their harvest.
Assign truth elsewhere.
Only the seasons matter.

Appoggiatura

Reality Is not the Supposition

The long wave breaks upon the beach in a greatening
   white,
The gull landing cries in ecstasy
Like Tarzan in bed with her for the first time.
As the heart,
The wave is only the force it loves
That carries it breaking,
A position only.
The gull squawks for refuse.
The fact of metaphor
Is the truth.

At the Ocean's Verge Again

Everyone on the beach carries the seeds of
                    generation,
Everyone. It is more than provision for ultimate
                    thanksgiving,
The mortal generosities are of wondrous
                    proportion:
Pitched footballs, frisbees caught
                    underleg,
High kites, all for joyfulness
                    like churchbells;
And something for something else: incessant
                    transistors,
Incorporated squattage and abandoned
                    beercans.
Tolerance is the lowest form
                    of goodness.
(*Helpless Jesus loves them, this*
                    I guess.)
I concentrate on a green and orange
                    striped
Umbrella and the fat girl emerged
                    from the ocean,
Her rubber elephant downside up,
                    the arriving
Wave coming waterworthy of jump
                    and joy.

On the Island of Torcello

Everything is eating everything:
It is not sufficient.
Five pilings at the wharf
Of the lagoon are crusted green
Where the waters wash—lush
Green, eager for the soft
Edible wood; the doge,
Foscari, set at table,
Dying of indigestion
At the age of 84—
And a cappuccino costs
Three thousand lire
At Harry's restaurant
On the island of Torcello
Where the greedy in mosaics
On the west wall of the cathedral
Boil in copper pots
While Mary on her toes
The other end blesses
The tourists drinking cokes
Under the moulding where Gabriel
Blows his windy blast.

I am definitely not up to it:
I order a four-minute egg
In Italian at the Osteria
Al Ponte del Diavolo
And get four eggs.

At the Lipari Museum

Twenty in two groups
Enter. The sun at the cemetery
Burns the stone, flowers
Cling to the wall crumbling
To shadows. Crests high
Above the doors look down
On the dead.

        Inside the building,
Painted jars stuck
Together (salamanders
Darting the grass) maintain
Erection.

        In the farther room,
Shards picked up in Lipari
And not in Hellas break up
The laughing gods.

        Gigglings
At the male amulets upstairs
Come down as I write
On the tomb-top.

At Urbino

Under the balcony of Montefeltro's
Garden the late cicadas
Cease.

I walk where the festival poster of Raphael's
Birth at the corner commends
Its faith

As the café with hard rock across
From the cathedral drags the silent
Moon.

Largo

Evening has fallen, the pylon-lights
Cross the water with points of gold, the tower
At St. Mark's breaks the line of shore.
Torcello is alone.
I turn to thoughts of cypress: Bellini's
Madonna holds from enmity
Her child, her restless Son.

For Yvonne Fletcher P.C.,
Died April 17, 1984

Caught in the present like an inadvertence,
I look with astonishment at the police cap
On the pavement of Sergeant Yvonne Fletcher
Shot down by Islam's hit-men
From the Embassy sill. The bullet went
In her groin. The prayer-mat's laid down,
The hindquarters raised in mercy.

> *All hip-hinges kept in good working-order*
> *All mosques kept in good working-order*
> *The pools floating cigarette-butts*
> *Eleven hit, one out of the way*

What I Mean by Goodness

When I am profoundly moved by goodness
My fourth finger goes numb,
Literally, the right-hand one,

Not from such ecstatic indulgence
As Berlioz' viola, Werther's
Noble brains blown out

And all the rest of it trailing self-made
Clouds of glory as Pip dies
Returning to heaven his home while

Literary bells bend. Nor
Elvis Presley's resurrected
Hips! Even Mother Teresa.

What goodness moves me is spontaneously there,
Like mumps, her dancing out
Of the bathroom with a sock in each hand in the
    pattern

Of the Union Jack (they can be bought
In the U.S.) to the helplessly inconsequential
Music of Schütt's *À la bien aimée*
On the stereo, drawn by the sheer hum of it.

An Elegy for Discourse

1   *The Irremovable Ut*

That blank which the printer includes
In the signatures to be corrected,
The page marked 'blank' at the front,
Is the ultimate poem, the purest—
But no fun. Words!
Bone-hoard, box, candle,
Retractable back to fact,
Testament of what is,
Mud, stone, god—

      an old shoe—the one
Van Gogh painted,
Brancusi's Bird in Space,
The filling in of ecstasy,
The tomb, a child forsaken.

2   *Of Exactness*

The decline of language mocks us.
Clarity! how else to what
We love? Fresh linen,
Who shaped your love of words.
The cold of a running stream
I think of—that clarity,
The right one for the particular hurt—
Whatever bread is lived by
No matter Jesus' gloom
Or Buddha's smile so long as
Good bakeries exist.

Loaves whose word is wheat.

3 Without Tongue in Cheek

Hypethral—usable word!
'Roofless' in its sound,
Open to the syllabic sky
As dictionaries are,
Those grand growling pointers
To the English tongue now left
On shelves suppliant to the music
And ineffable manipulations
Of the human tongue since
Cro-Magnon grunted.

      Anyway,

Hypethral or roofless be—
No attic rafters over you
But as those temples, Stonehenge,
Sounion, Segesta, that leave
Man's mind open to the starry
Skies, the crackling suns,
Dayspring or acronychal.

A History of Music

Gluck

Under the bee-buzzed sun
Willibald
lifts his wig
and pats his pate.

Mozart

Under the carpet
the two of them
discover
a gold florin.

Schubert

From the candle-bracket
wax drips down
to the closed keyboard.

Chopin at Majorca

With pincers
she lifts
a dead lizard
from the piano.

Liszt at Villa D'Este

The distant bells of Rome
mingle with the running
balustrades
and black cypresses.

Verdi

In the cave
at the back of the nunnery
the organist drinks
green poison.

Wagner

His wife was his aunt
his mother the daughter
of his wife's father.

Richard Strauss

Sex is bad, bad,
said John the Baptist's head.

Puccini

Swooning,
the diva loves
her little doll.

Debussy

A scarlet feather
touches
water,
Pan
starts.

Ravel

The swan dips his head
in a necklace of waters.

Stravinsky

The stuffing is out
at the seam
over the heart.

The Final Music

As in the *Schlummerlied*
Where the tonality is lost,
Liszt, his son dead,
His music unplayed,
Always on the move,
Pest, Weimar, Rome,
The old man, Europe
At his back, waits.

    Dark green the cypresses.

    His music "A room
    full of fumes," Hanslick wrote,
    The Cardinal Hohenlohe
    splendid in his scarlet robes,
    host at Villa D'Este,
    hears nothing.
    Wagner thinks only of himself:
        (Liszt's playing
        of the *Hammerklavier*
        that night at Wahnfried,
        Wagner in his nightshirt
        drawn out of his bedroom
        off the gallery above
        in sobs and ecstasy,
        displays the truth).
    Clara Schumann defending
    her husband, hostile,
    Brahms falling asleep at Weimar
    While Liszt played.

    The plaster fountains are turned off.

It is dark at four o'clock.

        Liszt Centennial, Washington D.C. 1986

1989
THE CELESTIAL CORKSCREW
& OTHER STRATEGIES

Postlude

Some of these poems were written to better the world, that is to say, outrageously. Quite a few of the poems are well ahead of the time in which they were written.

The dates vary considerably. Apart from formal indications, it is hard to tell. Human nature does not change; this in spite of the fact that the Church has added a few saints to its calendar and I have known poets who are humble. On the whole we have not overtaken Tamburlaine, Khomeini and some others who are born again and testify in glossolalia which is a hard language to determine. "We are built of corkscrews," says Sir Lawrence Bragg.

Some critics hold to the judgment that a light poem is not heavy. This judgment is not to be entertained.

R.G. 1988

On the Eve of Adam

They that are in the flesh cannot please God
— SAINT PAUL

The golden bough is broken, the moving sun
Draws up its waters from the stagnant pond
Once Jason knew.

That was nextdoor to Eden. Strange
How one tall tale usurped another, both
A pious fleece.

I take it no one nowadays would pledge
His future on a mutton's lights who knows
The price of chops.

Yet catechize these churches what they yean
That man should tremble at it, toss the salt
And damn delight:

Who wears this body wears a sin. Come.
A world condemned to grace a god and blackmail
Harps to heaven?

Can you contain this nonsense Adam is
A naughty love? morals not a matter
Of aesthetics?

At least it used to be the goatfoot god
Was glad, and every tumbled innocent
A snowy birth:

Presently, all five-sensed harbingers
Of love come swaddled with a cerecloth round
Their gorgeous dust.

I won't be sentimental either side—
But most devoutly beg the literate flesh
To hold its own.

Paeon of Bells for Lovers

Natural as rain and sunlight, limbs
   Only joys perplex;
Priapus and cool
   Euclid concocting sex:

O when this is, how the globe will spin!
   Gobi into park!
Coventry crowd its streets
   And Tom be out of work;

Shells and acorns legends be
   On oaks and golden sand;
Pools and mirrors smashed;
   Pulpits Samarkand.

Papal Paul who put the pants
   On Michelangelo
Shall roar him with Paul of Tarsus
   To doubled-up Jericho

While athletes tug the belfry ropes
   And virgin cornettes rage!
Jock shall have his Jill
   In that post-apple Age.

Lesson for Monday

Cynicism
can do things

Look at this wash hung on a line.
The whole truth's out.
Those male briefs, for instance,
            they
suggest something to you?
like longevity
        and transfiguration?
And that shirt
            that covers
        aspiration
            elongation   and
        consternation.

Mortality's suspended!
The sheet's a dead give-away!
Pyjamas wave
        I want
        to suspire
        with you.

Don't hand me that line

You mean myself?

Claire de Lune

There's nothing left
to compare it to—
time
tides
her who
Endymion kept,
repository of
leftovers
heirlooms.
But I know what it's good for

it has nothing to do
with listening to
Debussy
by

Optimistic Argument

There was no time despite
The lachrymals of those
Who've had it when this happy
Globe of apes and ant-hills
Didn't fumble forward
Schemes:

Straitly on his frantic
Mathematics works
Eliminating x;
Or, in the jungle rapturous
On his purple bottom
Dreams.

The adolescent moose
Among the lily pads
Has his heart's desire;
The joyful spider wraps
Her husband up in rearward
Web.

Odds are against it that
The clucking hen'll hatch
A peacock, the perfumed whale
Clear his throat. Yet Adam
Got a figleaf for his
Rib.

Or take the few who carried
That pacific motion
To debate at Dunkirk.
Did the Doctors get
A million angels on a
Pin?

The dandelions ope
Their golden eyes, the bat
At Heaven's bastion sings
And lovers all between
Their silken sheets are taken
In.

Ode for a Happy Event

Summer somersaults
Over into clover,
Beans pod,
Lambs frisk,
Clichés
Turn asterisks!

What sun is here
Is here by grace of her!
Storks pant,
Clowns wink,
Odds double.
Parentheses
Have trouble.

Between us we're triple.
Who knows? Quadruple!
Nurses rush
With warming pans,
Baby-buggies, bottles,
Doctors astrologian.

There's turmoil.
Joy turns turvey!
Interns watch,
Aunts wonder,
Computers jam and
Circumcisers ponder.

No wonder. no wonder!
The world's shoved off,
Bells sound
Noah's ark aboard!
Newton on the bridge,
Michelangelo
Aloft the ceiling,
Couperin and Rameau, furious,
Fourhands at the clavichord!

In the Big-Top

He juggles there
a zodiac:
slim knives
in hollow air

blade by blade
serrate on
the flashing air
shred sun

turn and turning
seek their zany's
single flaw
to flesh their yearning.

Above the love
of time, the wish,
death wheels,
craving flesh

that by a fluke
yet valid is:
earth, moon,
flaming rock—

hangs zenith, zed,
on clown despair
eyes fixed
on frightful air

where dance those daggers
utmost knives
whose scabbard is
his desperate love.

Chromatics

Sixteen basic hues
Holds Adam's eye,
Determinate by cones
Optically.

Disproven, red arouses
Chimpanzees;
Conically as cold
To it are bees.

Demonstrable by quartz
How far Wordsworth's
Rainbow would have
Fallen short;

Determinable how far
(By lens and rod)
Theotocopoulos
Distorted God.

Reducible in fact
To curves of air
Vincent's frenzied stars
And bedroom chair.

Inexhaustible world!
With skill, Eros
From dusty question
Possible!

In Zanipolo: Venice

I turned around
unexpectantly
and yes, there
was a saint
in silk robes
laid out in a glass casket
with a sliding cloth over it
pulled back now
it being high holy
holidays
and a cube of something
disinfectant or
dry ice to keep
the face from giving up—
the hands being gloved
in pink embroidery
it didn't matter
if they rotted a bit

I took one look and started
not because the corpse
was there and I hadn't
expected anything
certainly not a preserved saint
at my elbow
as I was looking up
at the monumental walls
the only start I got
when I got over the propinquity
of death behind me

was how
religion
had managed
to last so long.

The Minotaur Comes to Montreal

The balls
swung
as he lit out for the hills.
He was seated in a 315-hp Thunderbird Special
when I first saw him—
a bucket-seat Dyna Flow
filched from a stone house
on the Mountain.
He was going down Côte des Neiges.
I ran like hell
keeping up with the stop lights.
He had horns like a myth and the
bull's head
Europa rode behind—
Picasso had seen him all right.
I got caught up
at the intersection
of Peel and Ste. Catherine (the Kate
who lost her head
and was carried off by angels
to Mount Sinai;
Peel was very British).
A French-Canadian cop was trying to
give him a ticket.
I got there just in time
to see him take
one look at the two cultures
and give up the convertible.
It wasn't too good
his getting out that way
in the heart of Montreal.

One curate (Anglican)
forgot himself,
three nuns
had periods
and the milk chocolate in the
window of
Laura Secord's
amalgamated.
As I said,
he'd had enough. The last I saw
he was headed
down toward
the Sun Life Insurance building
across from the Cathedral.

In Dominion Square
the bulbs
all bloomed.

November 15, 1976

The cheering is always sad to someone.
In the streets the glorious hung on trucks,
Some blaring horns, some
Whistling girls, tilting from cans,
A bottle smashed in a corner,
The pavement sparkled.
Fleurs-de-lis waved.
Someone set fire to the maple leaf.
It was joyous, there was joy,
Canada dismembered.
Buildings lighted, the night filled
With joy, the whole was separate.
Upstairs, *parti* mouths
Orated, everybody
Reached for microphones. Culture
Was singular. Prophets
Spoke of greatness.
Some
Did not.

At the Jeu de Paume

Mankind
is *inexprimable.*
Here is this *expositeur*
Twenty-two with a beard
Expounding
The colours of Van Gogh,
Wearing dark glasses.

HAIKU
   —after a kakuyu print

The man walks by the flower.
Frogs slap their sides,
The hare rolls with laughter

EPIC
   —Sputnik 1957

A star
went by
with a dead dog
in it.

Zentralfriedhof, Vienna

Herr Potz maker of funeral urns
Works next door to Beethoven,
Brahms, Schubert, Wolf and all,
The best in Vienna—urns, that is—
Bevelled marble with handles and hoops,
Your name on it; inside, adequate;
Beautifully engraved, expensive, but that's
The way to live, *nicht wahr?*

Of course, Beethoven, Brahms & Co.,
Are not in expensive urns, they
Just lie there, all requirements
Filled, beating time, noting
Importances, major resolutions,
Great scopes and heart-leaps
While missing nothing humanly minor,
Requirements composed. Not needed
Potz' pots with beautiful handles.

Wagner Unbegrenzt

We took off our shoes in the opera,
It was Wagner,
Götterdämmerung
(The consonants are what to watch),
Four hours,
So I suppose it was all right.
Siegfried set out
In his wife's armour
(That is, his aunt's,
His mother was the daughter
Of his wife's father)
And got a spear in his back.
But our two feet were consonant
Each over the other—
Yours like a silk cat
Listening to a tuba.

Love Is for the Birds

I ran up three flights in the Library
Every fifteen minutes trying to get her
On the telephone. Promises are eyewash:
She would sit in all day, she said,
On the chance of seeing me. The Library murals
In the arches of the stairway are bad enough:
Eggheads standing around in high endeavour,
Females in white gowns offering virtue
To young men, I'd rather have the satyr
Erect in heat, done in busy red,
Studying Chloe cutting her toenails
In the bushes (yes, sweet Raphael drew it—
When he had time between Madonnas)
That was bad enough. I mean the stairways.
She was seated in a movie. I nearly
Wore the buffalo off four nickels
Trying to get her. I'll take up stamp collecting.

He Gets in Parentheses

She would rather take a nice hot bath and go
To bed. She had only worked eight hours, seen
Two operas (*Giann' Schicci* kicking up;
Salome disgusting at the well)
A morning dress rehearsal (she is crazy
About opera) parked her car (society
Demands all citizens on Wednesday move
Their vehicles on public streets from the left side
To the right) her hair was filthy and the circles
(From the opera) underneath her eyes
Looked like Euclid (the rinse she uses is called
L'aimant (loving it in French))
We could really then get really going
Before she had to take *Otello* in
(She was taking in *Otello* Thursday
On a ticket she had got) I said
OK, OK, I only offered love.

TV Award Night

Handed adoration, how
The glorious quiver,
Anticipations shiver!
Humble they take it,
The Oscar of yuk, the Tony of gunk.

Helpless with genius
They praise their wheaties,
Suppositories and duds.

May God rinse their reeking,
Throttle their larynx, plug up the suds.

Charge of the Light Brigade

Thistles and lizards, that's
What I got her into
Because of my stubbornness about
Knowing the way when I didn't;
Like Hannibal who lost fifty
Elephants choosing a wrong
Alp; Bonaparte and Moscow.
Sticking your neck out,
Charles on his royal block,
Is your own divine right—
It's your head. In my
Instance, alas, she was totally
Trusting, sweetly following
With the tote on her back wherever
My great pigheadedness
Led her, knowing it all.
Mountains look flat on a map.
Get yourself into lizards
And thistles but not your love.

The Sun Comes Out

Mr Watanabe of Japan had to tie down his holly tree
The winds were so high. They troubled the skirts of his wife
And ruined her umbrella. Mrs Watanabe is 72.
The winds were caused by a city industrial exhibition-hall
Far taller than the one-storey shops and private homes of
                              the Asakua district
Where Mr Koji Watanabe, the sandal maker, and his neighbours live.
Mr Watanabe is 80 years old. The winds and interrupted sunshine
Prevent his bonsai trees from bearing.
"I can no longer air my bedding quilts each day
And the washing won't dry outside," says Mrs Saku Watanabe
                              sipping her green tea.
The trash and litter swirl,
The housewives have to make detours when they go shopping.
Judge Izuri Kawarami awards Mr Watanabe and his neighbours,
Mr Sugisawa and Hiro Oto, six and one half thousand dollars damages.
"Sunshine is essential for a comfortable life," he rules.

Ars Poetica

i
Pomes
Aren't tomes:
On hers and his
The emphasis.

ii
The poet is
Viz:

A man
Who can
can the oil
And oil the can

(Not
God wot
A goil
Who can)

He
Can be
The sert
Of man
Who is the squirt
And yet the can

A poet can

Figurations

Cinquains of a Sort for E.P.

Ezra who ate two tulips while Yeats intoned
   Took a tuck in the style of the Oirishman.
He kept petals from withering!
   Young trimbeard, turquoise in ear,
Kept poems from slithering!

Done before he died, said poet Graves:
   "Bloomsbury litter." Moon his pin-up, he scaled
The thundered Theban wall!
   No Capaneus; kept
Apricot blossoms from fall,

Constructed Iliads . . . All the way to Venice
   Bus by bus and train to catch a glimpse of him,
Rome to Ravenna, thence
   Down the Canal. At seventy and
Nine, not a chance—

Ez at Spoleto spouting his opera and verse . . .
   Now derry-down-derry, dead! Ah well, he's there
In his book, old miracle of the metre,
   More shape in a phrase than anyone's,
Beauty durable, completer!

For Bill Williams

It was one of those immortal wounds
Mister Frost talks about

a poem

sixteen words
it was made of

concerning the value
of a 1923 wheel
barrow

I was struck dumb
anything modern
could last
so long

Words with Basil Bunting

Music has its own meaning.
What is your meaning, sound?
You knew. Both!
Beowulf is rough
Plato tough.
Can't get around that.

Music thinks sensuously,
Thought is sensuous in music,
That's the strife with you,
You want to be
Scarlatti or what you don't like,
Wagner and his gold E$^{\flat}$.

In syllables meaning is:
Fact is no pedant's game.
Grass caught in willow
Tells the flood's height the water gone.

The slowworm's got his motif.
Starlight quivers.

odditorium

while
s(knowing)ly
mister
   ee!
cummings says
his poems &
springtime busts
right out
(all over)
May
from each
enthus ee!
astic clap
p ing f
   ee!
male   god!
grace us all

Ned Pratt Lowered

Here's a farewell to you, Ned!
How many of us have you fed
In your time there at York
On roast beef, lamb chops, pork,
Trimmings before and after, gin
To wash the titan evening in,
Postprandial whiskey, rum, and port
To land us half-seas over short
Of nothing? Not a man of us not
Your dearest friend. Dashedly caught
Up with you, have they, Ned, that tide,
Those monuments of ocean? complied
Have you? Gone, eh? By God,
I hear that genial laugh and broad
Beamed moon-faced loving lilt
Of the voice of you: lads, lads; the tilt
Of the head as you say it. No tide will take
You out. You're here with us. Make
Merry, Ned. You've got your two
Slabs on a hill. We'll not mourn you.
No elegy. You defeat
Us with your angled boards, complete
And uttermost, grace given
Out, the last spike driven.

F. R. Scott

To say
that this man is fantastic
is to be
Frankly wrong.
Real
is the right root
for him.
He bears history,
the lakes
he dives under,
the cold hard sun
he walks in,
Canada, perhaps.
He shoulders
distance,
levels
facts.
Nothing is too true
for him.
Praise
he goes into,
padlocks
he gets well out of
and piety.
He chairs children
and keeps up wit.

Not to say
if this man is
God is.
Mortality
moves him,
he goes for wrong-doing,
never lets bad enough
alone.
Being with him
is not psalm-
singing
but pfun.

Words
he gets the wear out of,
lives by a poem,
buried with respectable honour
goes
Scott-free.

Arthur Smith

Wandering around
With portly bearing,
Restless, the half-full
Glass in your hand,
The room as though
A cage of knowledge
Hitched with shadows,
Answering with quips
The inevitable, you
Are poet. All
Come to knowing,
None with more
Aptness, who've licked
Dying and still
Face it. "I've made
My contribution,"
So you say,
knowing full well
You have to keep
On making it,
Nothing knowing,
Old Jelly Roll
Your immediate pan-
acea, Death
Still the more accurate
Archer.
    Suddenly,
You have to go home:
To lift Smoky
From the thunderstorm,
The dog not able
To rise, being
Old and arthritic.

Letter for Earle Birney

Cammina, cammina, la morte e vicina!
You know what Boito knew—you
Of the last of the mountains—22 storeys up,
The whole of Toronto a shatter of lights
All over night, the longitudes curving,
The rounding globe a web of them swiftening north
To the dredge of that gravity no man can hold hard in mind,
Calgary, Vancouver, Anian, to the final
North, still point of the still centre;
London, Athens, Fiji, crossed
On their longitudes at the still point of the slanting
Pole: *La Morte*. Well may Mefistofele
Stand half-akimbo caressing his waxed moustache,
Purple lights and hissing this side
The proscenium while the maestro drops his pince-nez
In the score. *Comédie humaine*!
   Death? yes, *currite noctis equi*.
Night stars are beautiful over Massawippi.
Each night they are many and beautiful—as
They were when you were here—and I have yet
To learn their silver disposition. *Terminat
Hora diem*; *terminat auctor opus*.
You write of me: "The best damn poet in Canada."
No matter you were in your cups. I dot my i
With diamond. With your words I halt indifference.

              I write this
Sprezzatura, knowing you are there
In Toronto, writing poems, falling out of trees,
Writing *con amore* and beating death.

John Glassco

You babbled unstutteringly of stocks and bonds
In the kitchen here where years later you wept
Because Elma was unkind, poor dear,
With her sloped sporting hat in the white sporting
Convertible. She did not know what she was saying
There in bed in the Montreal Hospital. Money
And years of love, you had them both, I suppose,
Though your poetry hardly exposed either.
There you stood, gin and orange juice,
A friend of worth though I never knew exactly
What was worth you were friend to. Dividends
And profit surprisingly as managed as your formal verse.
Anyway, your advice was no good.
I do not understand money. Your poetry
I did though, as finished as Beau Brummell.

    Buffy—as stuffed with sardonics as his catbird.
I think you were genuine. Hard to tell.
I see you ensconced in the Sloan leather chair,
Pink in the face, giggling quietly, no one of us
Ever knew at what. Now, over
A tumbling stream in Foster, your ashes taken
In by the waters—anonymous, with ascot at
Your throat and a crystal wine glass in your hand,
Inscrutably amused—as you would have it.

The Unquiet Bed

Fond Lord imperious!
This is serious.
This woman would claim us,
Defame us.
Her heart is set
Because we sweat,
Nature is
Musculature.
She'd lay us,
Waylay us,
Preferably on stubble.
We have trouble.
Our chins are tired
Projected as required
To laborious dawn,
Socially marching on.
We want to lie down
Without renown,
Sweet consolations,
Tribulations?

Irving

This man, grandiloquent,
Boastful,
Humble before goodness,
As the tumbling night,
The aerobatics of sun,
Foolstruck
In the glory of rage,
The astonishment of words,
Like Joshua, commands
Contradictions,
That all negatives
As those walls
Be brought down.

Eurithe Purdy's Battered Coffee-Pot

That battered coffee-pot in Kiev—
Sovietskaya, was it?—and the poems!
Those breakfasts of glub, drabness
Excelling, pomp, chandeliers, carpets,
Pedestals, and the bathtub running mud!
That cockeyed typewriter borrowed
From Igor Petrovich, Cyrillic innards
That wouldn't strike, Al pecking out
Comedy across the hall, me
Deciphering hungers, and Eurithe's battered
Saving Grace, God bless it, all.

On Exchanging Collected Poems with Ray

Your poem "Ersatz" forty-five years ago—
And mine you wished me good ease for. Music
In an anxious world: wondering "why it's no good,
No good any more, no good at all."
Later Prague and Lidice, parameters.
Only the names change of power and hurt.

Half a century writing them! What folly
To think that could alert indifference:
The living instant of the poem's rage.
And yet, the silent increment, the answer made.

D. G. Jones

He turns the wilderness
into a few petals

his poems
join spaces
between bells

a stone
is joy

the rose on its green stalk
accounted for

is blood
in a far country

Flakes of snow
are small birds
in spring

in the crevices
water runs silently
and the grass
has answers of notable calibre

a seed

in the hurricane's
still centre

Postscript

In Memoriam A. J. M. Smith and John Glassco
1980 and 1981

Buffy and Art,
I don't know if—no—
We won't see them again—
Arthur with his tumbler of martini
Wandering, getting the gossip,
His poems polished till they shine
Like Brancusi,
And Buffy whom the two of us stopped off to see,
Art driving two-wheels-aside crazy every curve
To the clapboard house,
Buffy, horseman among farmers;
Polished his verse, too, formal as a
Four-in-hand, a glass of Beaujolais
(Something odd in the offing,
The bathroom done in black)
Grace and the silent chuckle
At the chewing gum on the Parthenon—
And A.J.M. in his outboard tearing up off Drummond Point
For news of the phoenix!
That they'll come again,
How could it be?
Classic shade and a point of sky
Over Memphramagog, Brome,
Both hating death.

Epitaph

Astrophysicist
And Ferencz Liszt
He wanted to be.
He settled the matter
With poetry.

NOTABLE NOTE

For the poem, "On the Eve of Adam," please contemplate Paul's statement to the Romans 8:8 and take into consideration "the sinful flesh" 8:3.

For my "Paeon for Lovers" consult the same propoundments and carefully consider I Corinthians 6:18 and 7:9. Daniele da Volterra 1559 following the injunction of Pope Paul IV painted pants on Michelangelo's nudes in the Sistine Chapel and thus achieved immortality.

1991
SHADOWS IN THE GRASS

But no more of this blubbering, now,
we are going a-whaling.
— HERMAN MELVILLE

Out of the Seasons All Things Come

The House Fire

The piled boards burn catching
In the snow. The perimeter of soil
Grows, spreads in discolour.
Somebody is burning an abandoned house.
Smoke lifts above the firs,
The green-smelling hemlock. The yellow
Blue-centred flames adjust
To the empty spaces. Snow
Begins to fall. Flakes touch
Fire.

        Remembrance is futile.
It brings back death for selection.

        The heat is too much.
I turn from the blaze. A red
Slash goes out. The snow falls
Heavily where the boards burn.

The Abundant Earth

Everywhere you look life goes crazy.
A hummingbird is in the clover,
A brown lily has come out above
A bush holding what looks like
Burrs sprouting scarlet buttons.
A bug is nesting.

Even where you can't look:
In the interstices of the Pyramids,
Stones so perfectly fitted, they said,
They keep out life: kitchen stuff
Interrogates the strictest structure.
Bases crumble.

Plankton for whales! Outrageous assignment!
Ticks in fur, water-holes in Sahara,
The shove of love endows the emollient
Oyster; bookworms. It's crazy.
What the earth is for and why
I leave to fossils.

Amusement of God. My guess is chemistry.
I have written before that the earth
Teems. So it does. Sitting
Under the smell of fumbling lilacs,
Eating a homemade sandwich,
I say it again.

Out of the Seasons All Things Come

Seed breaks sides, the fern uncoils,
Across the wall signatures spring.
Slogans assail the day with sumptuous
Flaws, astringent students study
Luxurious laws, governments falter
In their provision. The heart proclaims
In many ways. On fortunate isles
Temples tilt their ruined bells.
The last of the condors lays an egg.
Documents hatch. Wonders spread.

The ocean rolls.

Laurence Sterne a-dying put up
His hands as if to stop a blow.

Observe How

Everything is busy in nature, even
The stationary fish gulping
Ingests invisibilities. The famished
Ant is frantic in the grassblades. There's
Obsession for you! The grids of earth
Collide. Too far north, the magnolia
Tries to bloom. The flooding river
Pushes leaves.

Learning is at work.
Our galaxy is a quarter smaller than
We thought it was. Did you know?

The marrow-bone hides what it knows.

Take the Unanswerable, for Instance

The AIDS virus knows how to replicate
Itself, so does the simplest dumb cluck
Laying eggs or Cleopatra in heat.
Free will is no explanation. Faith,
Heaven help us, is all we have to fall
Back on, that answers everything
That isn't there, insistences that are—
Fingers dipped in the font as we leave.
Faith denied, where would Chartres be?
Caught in the crossfire, what to settle for?

Nothing when you get down to it.

Ignorance, ritual doubled on a mat
Three times a day the floor overhead.
The prospect is unsettling. Promulgations,
Probables, or sundry flowers picked
In May . . .

So passed the day, so
Passes all impossible loves and answers.

One Has to Pretend Something Is Amused

Death in a taxi going from here to there
Instead of staying put pursuing truth
In the kitchen or up in the attic or somewhere,
Perhaps making love or pulling up weeds
In the garden which is far safer and less trouble
Later on. However, one must be
In movement to sell goods and converse with the world.
Hazard is inevitable. Too bad if the heart
Gives out and the driver has to dispose
Of an unwanted corpse but he turned down the flag
On his meter and so must take a chance as well
On being responsible or not.

On the whole it seems best not to make
A move. Though here again who can judge
When the kidneys and liver will shut down
Or in the statistically likely case I spoke of,
That of the arteries to the old pump? I wouldn't
Want to be alone in any case but probably
Will be, two loves and death
Never coinciding.

A tip ready for old Charon poling
Your ghost across the river Styx would be
Appropriate. You know the Greek myth? Never
Mind. Take your earthly taxi to where
You are off to. Destiny will be as much amused,
Lack of understanding won't matter.

And Yet

To have one's life add up to yet
— RANDALL JARRELL

What else could there be, this intricate
Body ours, less and more
Assigned to choose from?
      (O free will!)

The careening cosmos is a mixture.
So are we. What a fluency
Runs through the vessels
      To the heart,

Fragility, wear and finish! Memory
Also has sorrow for its end.
Yet indeed!
      The whole of this round

And global is a yet! Adam
Who ate apples lost his love,
Yet I found mine
      In '56.

Chance a basis for a choice!
Thus—you know the rest. There's none.
So we talk better
      Than the whales?

We observe ourselves: I add balance
To stumble, tomorrow to the past—both
Superior to a *yet*—
      Yet . . .

The Reversal

The cosmic intention:
To mock conclusion . . .

The close of day,
the empty road,

That distant bird
Of notable song

Which has stopped singing.
Mockery is validation.

Of Chopping Wood and Codas

They all end, woodfires and symphonies,
All of them, nothing is worse than each
Finished if you love music and are cold
By nature, not much on your bones,
Codas come to. Indignation
Flatters, but that is graveyard whistling.

      As you get on though,
      Humility is silly.

What I do is shape words
All night and get up late.
Chopping wood also fools
One. The Kaiser chopped cords of it . . .

The Planet on the Edge of Nowhere

Insignificance is what troubles the world.
Without virginity wedded who is she?
Napoleon killed two million people—
Take one or two. Look at the American Eagle
That flags its wings, Miss Universe unfurled.
Saint Simeon sat on a pole.

    Love finally gets to those who leave
Something of worth, but obscurity's the passion, no one
Wants it, particularly those who yell loudest.
Prominence is what matters—Peary at the pole,
Judas who didn't rejoice at suppertime,
The March Hare's tea party.

So It Seems

I am awake at the margin of morning:
The shutter blurs the sun: the flower
Is in the glass at the edge of the table:
The ceiling is in order. It is clear
The letter posted shouldn't have been.

     Cutlery makes a noise . . . Jerusalem
Is in turmoil again.

               Two warnings.
He always blows two warnings
At the level crossing, the engineer.
Having to at some time,
I will not go downstairs. Easter
Is another day.

        So it seems.

Winter Solstice

The rake leans against the side
Of the house. Thick snow lines
The length of the cedar hedge, the path
To the house has feet of it. Rake and snow?
Something is amiss. The tricky squirrel
Runs up and down the vertical tree and
All's in balance. Not with the world,
As everyone knows. *Adieu, forêt,*
Tchaikowsky's Joan of Arc sang.
Acid, the rain. The Lorelei
Has moved from the factory spill. No more
Consonance, no more trees and fish.
Rake and snow! Poor winter solstice.
Cough, cough. You'd think it would
Have been a shovel. No matter.
All will be answered come spring:
Cranberry juice is antacid.
The shortest night of the year will swing round.

At the Twenty-First Century

Of Existence

Around Saturn the thousand rings
Not there until we saw them,
Seventeen moons undone without us.
Out of the dross of time all
Is particular. A thousand coloured rings
Ring the heavens our wit makes palpable.
Titan is. Hyperion is.
We have walked on the moon.
The brooding whale is numbered, whole
Species are accounted for.
Shout *Jubilate*. Modestly.

At the Twenty-First Century

The ozone layer around the earth punctured
By a can of aerosol. That's about it.
The end. We'll all fry. So says the report
Filed by the agency. Antarctica
Has a big whole over it. She who lies
In the sun will get cancer . . .

                            Temporarily.
The heart's transplanted. The arm sewn on again.
Software will lick the problem. Man
Loves his neighbour with all his little heart.

Episode in Quilalí

The way the children look into the open coffin
argues well for the next episode:
they look at the victim killed by a land mine
which tore through the bus he was riding in,
with usual composure, perhaps a curiosity
not yet exhausted but nothing to interfere
with any call to necessary violence that may come—
certainly compassion won't interfere; the boy,
arms folded, looking and not particularly
concerned, is sufficient augury. The momentum
toward the right life will go on.

> This was in Quilalí, Nicaragua,
> But it could go on anywhere, the premise
> Is still good though confined at the moment
> To Central America. Mr Ernst Zundel of Toronto,
> Canada, for instance, says the Holocaust
> Is a hoax perpetrated by Jews to extort
> Reparations from Germany.

It is hard not to throw up—coffins and ovens—
but one must stick to one's last with eyes on the goal
here and there and thus prevent enlargement.
We can't go around hugging each other.

Valentine's Day 1988

Argument

Dolphins will leap, elephants sing,
When the world comes to its senses.
You care for these things? Song?
Elephants? Change is the crux, not
Simplicities otherwise inefficient.

Trees Mostly

Grace and Pretend, kids and carrousels happy,
And all the rest of the sentimental world.
Green, the world's provision! Green trees!
Leafy text.

                      The parrot abandons Brazil,
The redwoods fall, reality survives.

                Courtesy toward a forest?

The Way of the World

I am far away and gamelan music
Goes on whether I am in Bali
Or not.

That Rameses' statue colosally stands
At Abu Simbel and I deteriorate
Is funny.

All these years Niagara Falls
Falls, ever roaring, ever
Roaring.

Those lovers Abélard and Héloïse
Draw tourists to the cemetery
In Paris

But I am in love. Despite free will,
The homeless at dusk ready their cardboard
Boxes.

                    etcetera, etcetera.

All this goes on as I sit here,
Each quota waits, each quota
Waits.

News of the Day

A brief runover: the executive
Delegates authority, the inquiry
Becomes the inquired.

Toddlers aim guns,
Tanks collide on the nursery floor,
Bang, bang!

Mobs are better, numbers
Satisfy, quantity works,
Restrictive quotas.

The World Solved

The need is an Absolute to go on,
Prismatic Light, a First Principle
To hold onto, then all is simple,
Even in elaboration.
Furious April supplies this,
The air so rinsed with love, we love—
Counterpart of that hair-raising
Absolute—not the Word itself
But proof enough:

                all these come-ons,
Seasons the world leans against,
Sortable worships and kingdoms come—
Equivalent muddle and joys
Such as ducks in a pond, a drink
Of water, even that elemental!
Our senses deal in these things.

The need is irreducible wonder.
Empty planets circling a sun!

One Way Out

Beyond perjury lies the poem
(*Lies?*). Facts are what for,
What poetry hawks in handcarts
And makes accessible, which is to say,
Meaningful: Noah going
Groundward, the bottom well stowed,
The riding in accord with natural bumps
And laws; life such as a man
Falls in love with and is immediately
Himself. Job hammering planks!
Saint Anne once, so it is said,
Inhaling a rose conceived Mary.

A Window Lighted

A Window Lighted

The house across the road turns dark.
The hedge, the trees against the sky
Turn dark.

It is winter. One night and a barren
Road and a house silent since
This morning

Become great consideration.
Snow, the fall of all one night,
A light,

A moment unaccounted for,
Is turned on and the heart is moved.
No

Consternation of facts commending
Desolation has contradiction against
Nearness:

The up-hill road impassable,
Small foraging marking access
Only—

The hedge a snowfall higher if
You must, April brought no nearer—
The roadside

Window of a house comes on
And the world is changed with possible
Love.

Somewhat of Lilacs

1 *The Weather Was Consistently Cold*

Nothing was there on the bush, at least
The clenched green went unnoticed, the weather
Too consistently cold for anything to be expected.
One gets conditioned by cold in the bones
And things extraneous: the pathetic
Martyr draped in flags, the moving
Uninformable infant without
Food—a far cry from lilacs.

      Yet there they were, there they were,
The sudden white sweet-smelling double lilacs.

2 *The Storm Mounts Then There Was Sun*

Each year the lilac bends with double blossoms,
The scent of branches on the sidelong air.

April, late April, is the testament. Autumn,
Moon, tides, we know all about.

An hour now the rain will knock blossoms down—
Clouds are thickened, the wind east, with thunder . . .

It is over. The torn branch from the lilac
Is at the step. Motionless the distant trees,

The foliage wet with rain. Evening falls.
Where the corner of the house stands,

A patch of racing sky and stars
Is defection, over the garden where

The brief moment is, the influential
Moon, for all its waiting tides, enhancement.

Nightjars

One judges with something like acceptance
Now the past gives way to wisdom.
Vanished tides have never been,
Summers are their autumn leaves . . .
Tomorrows come at a quickening pace
Turning assertion to yesterday;
Quickening swallows in the evening air
Are elegy.

Irony predicts experience:
April is the April lost,
The hastened snow banked at the road
Loudening the stream, the crescents
Of frozen apples where they scattered
Fell—each departure where
The lingering winter meets the sun,
Is verdict.

I walk the galaxy. The supernova
Brightens; out of fire, falls in and
Worlds begin. I'm still as constant—
Good sole amandine, a Riesling
With it. I am for embodiment,
This cosmos jocular polishing
A halo: abstract gravity's
Not good enough.

I said this years past, most of it.
Sheer percipience forced to the conclusion,
I look out of that bedroom window
Of years ago, each dusk the same,
Shadows cut by the nightjars, wings
Slant, the only sound, passing
Questions seeking night, their harsh
Cry.

Birds

Nothing exceeds the beauty of the redpoll
Landed in snow, the bank by the porch
Where the alder catkins are forage for winter.

This is the hour, this is the day
That will do, when the soul comes up
Against ecstasy, common skirmish,
Ordinary deifying.

They flash like strokes of gods, the birds.

At the Jungfrau

1

I suppose the heavenly gates swing outward
And aerialists see there equivalents
Of what we have on athletic earth
Of worth and wear and love and coming
Spring? We are sadly here,
Yet (for all the gloom and doom)
Make as insistent stands and breathless
Landings as any performed in heaven.

2

Hereabouts is real business,
A gorgeous heartbeat ahead of heaven,
Death too soon to solve the love of it.
Health knows this, at least
The well enough who look at the clock
And count their toes. Watch the dying
Who pluck their blanket not letting go
As if they wouldn't abandon earth.

3

The sun shone that day out
On the Jungfrau. We talked of love and mountains;
Of lost chances most likely. The sun
Snagged on a ridge of ice; tipped
Over; then was gone—the way
Life goes. It got colder at once
(Naturally!). We discussed regret as well,
But it didn't seem to matter. Not much.

4

Have you walked along that monastery corridor
Of tombs, the lids off—near Burgos,
Isn't it?—straw and a chicken brooding
Inside one. *Cluck, cluck.*
We were startled ourselves. Within the chapel
The abbot was laid out in braid and velvet.
No more. Vamoosed. Not any more.
Cluck, cluck. Yes indeed.

5

At Lourdes the halt and sorrowful wait
For their transformation. By all means!
(Short of what can be got cheaper
In plastic saints and electrified Virgins).
We thought of this among the mountains.
The worth of superstition is mightily
Present among crevasses and snowpeaks.
It's the sense of how high is height.

6

If you take one of the aerial lifts
From Grindelwald to the upper meadows
You can get to heights that are dazzling;
I mean, the worldly colour transcendent
From the valley below, flowerings
Red and crimson, purple, white,
Walked on. A mile in is Bachsee,
A clear lake of significance—or not.

7

We still picture that afternoon
Among the snowpeaks. Then
Two girls came up over
The fenced ridge (we are back sitting
Among those glaciers above the Jungfrau
Valley). They didn't stop talking.
I believe they are going to invent plastic
That naturally destructs . . .
O wayward world!

The Lovers

The hills darken in the setting sun,
The strip of cloud is crimson in the sky,
Then is gone . . . blue, the water
Is blue at the far reaches from such
Sun as the hills allow, the heavens
Exceeding as the stars appear. Two
Lovers have only themselves where the gradient
Goes up to the trees. Cars go by.

It is against reason that the stars
And world take precedence.

Love Poem

I hardly see you in the opposite room,
The *Times*, part of Sunday's *New York Times*,
Held up before you—a glimpse of the pale-blue
Cardigan, the crimson slacks, your knees raised
Before the well of the desk, these colours only . . .
The endless print! News of the world between
Sales of unprecedented proportion. On the desk
Gladiolas, slashes of fire!

                    I almost went on
Describing. I want belief in this. Too many
Adjectives, adoration. Well enough alone.

Interlude

Breathing softly as I listened to Delius,
My love slept. The sun touched
The soft pillow, orange beneath the window,
Her head below on the softness, one arm
Underneath her cheek, rounded apple colour,
And I thought of Adam's Eve,
He allover dirt trying to dig houseposts,
And of death,
One year her or myself alone. But now,
The sun, slanting westward,
Caught through the green glass bottle
On the sill of the small upper window
Where it was as she had placed it,
Death not right away
But near enough. I listened and
Delius' music of its own shortness,
Soft and passionate in its way,
Ended.

        She moves,
Hearing the silence . . .

                my heart again beat,

Watching where she lay

Shadows in the Grass

Observation is no good—the glimpse
Out the window at the irrelevant lawn.
I leaned, kissed the back of her neck
There at the window. Out of impulse
I walked to her and bent down.

Reference brought distortion.
Autumn leaves from the rain outside
Were on the grass.

Complexity is
Aside from love: equatorials,
Remembrance in a book,
Tomorrow. I bent down
At mortality's edge.

Love Statements Instated

What if "silken" define
Her hair? imply
Mortality?

A truer thing:
Death denied
Its exultation.

Moon and Snow

Well, that's the way it is,
Love and particulars
In moderation.

Sometimes it is just as political
To look up and find
Happiness in locations

Neither first nor last
In the world such as
Trees and fences

In focus, sun on the edge
Of the hills, the moon
On white snow.

Tuscany to Venezia

Tuscany to Venezia

1

The vines on their trellis claim the sun,
Fields of sunflowers, wagons
In numbered July—

The rows laid down, the harrowing done—
The hot work, a labour
Loved—parishes

Of roots, calendars of wine!
Tuscany where Buonarroti
Chose his marble

Out of Carrara and Donatello
Dropped his apron of eggs
Starting in wonder

At Cimabue's Jesus nailed.
Schifanoia at Farrara,
Fresco of joy,

Hand at his lips Goodbye—where
In all this sunburned land
No meanness is found.

2

Except at Florence. People
Dislike one another,
The impregnable streets
Apportioned.

Discoloured in dust in the Medici
Chapel, the Duke of Urbino
Poses Why
(The way

Michelangelo put
That hand of his, the back
Placed on the hipbone
Sideways),

Friendship a commerce.
Pleasant it is to sit
In ignorant places
Elsewhere.

3

In San Donato at Murano
(The floor of the nave inlaid
With peacocks and labyrinth)
What we come to, a sarcophagus,
Is a font at the door.

4

Because of the crowd descended with cash
And an hour in Venice, one queues up
At the Bridge of Sighs to get across.
There are other walks. On the Dorsoduro
The many cul-de-sacs are endless,
Like sepulchres, but Ruskin found
No confusion as he made his way
Along the Zattere to St Mark's cathedral
Whose five hundred pillars, porphyry, jasper,
Are useless, holding up nothing but beauty.

5

Beauty has
Possibilities.

6

Aesthetics! Gigli singing
Bizet's "Fisher of Pearls" on an
Old phonograph record

In Vasari's loggia at Arezzo,
The antique dealer listening shows us
Gooseflesh come on his arms!

What happiness! the customers everywhere,
The sunny hills holding grapes
And graveyard cypresses!

Piero of the frescoes thrived here
And Romano who drew a dozen
Ways, his drawings explicit.

7

At Gimignano, who had the highest
Tower had the noblest house.
The ascension had to be stopped by statute,
51 metres, no more. Little
Saint Fina reached heaven carried
By angels. Others tried something else.
Pisa carted shiploads of earth
From Calvary to cover the Cemetery, Verona
Elevated tombs outdoors,
Siena took up racing horses.

8

The prevarications of impossibility!
They built palaces on water, crazy
But exquisite,

Stabled four bronze horses
On the balcony of the cathedral forefront.
Why not?

The four oligarchs in porphyry
Hug each other overcome
At the far corner.

The versatility of exculpation!
Every year at Redemption the Venetians
Have fireworks.

9

Blesséd be the Goths who pushed
The Venetians onto these islands!
Torcello, abandoned for greatness,
Venezia absolute,
Between East and West a thousand
Cargoes wedded to the seas,
Here, water
Sustains marble.

It is the light, the light,
Of poets, makers of music,
Painters,
Uncompromisable light—light on waters
That takes the heart
As life does . . .

La vecia! glistening
On a bedroom ceiling,
The barge of oranges below.

10

Repentance and doom, the monk preached.
They listened. The eloquence promised heaven—
More—God come down on earth.
The golden-haired Raphael listened.
Venus on her cockleshell,
Drawings of love's slavery,
Wrinkled on the preacher's fire.
Alas, alas, rubies, jewellery,
The crocheted collar on her velvet
Gown, were fuel
For the purging flame.

Him, the *civitas* burned. A small
Plaque in the square marks the spot.

A few cells down from Savonarola's,
Blesséd Fra Angelico
Painted the Annunciation
On his knees. A stone's throw
Across the street, in the Galleria
Uncircumcised David stands naked.
The queue can hardly get in.

11

It may be that the Church is ossified
But it consoles the simple.
I stand in line to mount
The Sacristy steps to the reliquaries
And view in a glass case
The lower jaw of Saint Anthony.

The wristbone of Saint John
Is on display at Topkapi
In Istanbul.

One might get a whole skeleton.

12

The angel swinging his feet in happiness
Seated on Jesus' tomb can be found
On the bronze doors of Pisa cathedral.

13

The bell tower leans,
Good Fridays mourn.
Poor Ugolino
Buried alive with all his sons.
Some word is needed about that
On Easter days.

14

Each walks round as if
His flesh was his. What
If each consulted his bones?
Galileo with his stars,
Ghiberti and his doors,
Giotto his tower, each
Loaned what was his.

15

Only the loser
Inherits the world.

16

And a red round low down full
Moon came up behind the Church
Of the Redeemer across the lagoon
As we ate ice cream at Nico's.

17

Extravaganzas! But out in the country
(Slow, the Arno to the sea)
Red strawberries,

Buried truffles, mamma with
Geese and the wash and the drying
Sheets on a bank.

In Santa Maria dei Miracoli,
Tucked away in a side-chapel
Bellini's Madonna and young son.

18

They are going to restore Miracoli.

19

To the side of the Medici Chapel—all
Of Michelangelo's tombs outdone
By the love in his Mary
For the unfinished Child.

20

Colour and fluency, Tiepolo's art!
The rhetoric of Veronese,
Tintoretto's flying hulks,
Venetian vulgarity.

Far cry the corner where the Ca' Foscari
With the lantern is—elegance!
And sweep up the courtyard stairs where
Othello did!

21

Truth is the thing.
Poor Desdemona,
A willow song.

Interment limited on San Michele:
Twelve years, a corpse;
Bloody Colleoni
On his monument.

22

I watch the curious go up and over
At the Ponte Sepolcro.
No let up.
The kid howls amid the legs and steps.
No escape, youngster.

23

Well that's about it, an end
To the endless—
As much as can be said if
You are inclined otherwise:

For sitting in the bow of the *vaporetto*
Across the lagoon (Route 1)
Without a thought of anything
But water and sun and the going.

24

One thing more.
Melone can be bought
At the corner of the Campo San Maurizio
And *prosciutto di Parma* to go with it
On the Salizzada di San Lio.

In the Church of Vivaldi, Venice

1

Listening to Vivaldi with Half-Appreciation

Up and down the scale with ornaments.
Embellishment—that was the thing,
Music in a wig—nicely curled
And powdered—each note where it should be,
The mode proper, *largo* for gentle
Death, *roulades* for ladies a-horse,
Piu allegro for getting there.

All is baroque here in Santa
Maria della Pietà—Vivaldi's trio
Too delicate for the space, the flautist
Cherubic in the blowing, the oboe
Showing off, alas, the cembalist
Getting old, his cheekbones
Prologue to another and better world—
Up and down the scale in minor
Mode—but Tiepolo on the ceiling!
Fooling the eye with major progressions,
Vaultings so you can't get to him.

Outside,
Hawkers; *gruppetti* within. So
It is, this sleepy concerted evening.

2

Six Concerti per Violino e Orchestra

The same, all six! Yet a lively fellow,
This Vivaldi heard again
Each season, September this time,
Venice chilly and winterward—
In the chancel angels that can't fly
Shivering in gilt trying to get to
Tiepolo's *trompe l'oeil* ceiling
Where it's lively with joy and love.
'*Scusi* Vivaldi! a good enough fellow
Though caught in your replicate century
Major to minor at the appropriate sigh,
But one sermon far too many!

Two Landscapes with Figure

Southernly, Tuscany loved by poets
And other measurers of the soul—
A Renaissance of painters sun and
Saints in their head! North, Canada,
Land of complacence, snowcrests,
Space to the Arctic in their brain.

Grapes sun-imprisoned. Long
Thoughts before a winter fire.

Theodoric imperial in his opened tomb
Blown away . . . crusty kegs
At Ravenna, the Ca' de Ven . . . From the eaves,
Imperious icicles night-stars
In them forgotten by June . . .

But that
Guy carrying skis at the corner
Of San Trovaso in the heart of Venice!—

What world? One?

The Final Scene

It is a kind of grandeur at the end.
— WALLACE STEVENS

In the Rezzonico Palace—a room
Rented to die in—Browning, knowing
The last. his Elizabeth in mind, his Italy.
Midmorning goes by, the Canal
Slapped by movement; at the sharp corner
The gondolier-cry; the outboard barge
Driven, heavy with crates and hardware
From Mestre.

        Venice and remembrance! melons, August,
Evenings, the light shattering across
To the Salute steps where we sit, saints
Behind us, the day next nowhere near . . .

Projections and Homilies

Oh, Another Dozen Profound Stanzas

1

Conditions were such that the world
Was snow, white, everywhere,
On red chimneys, exposed
Noses, clotheslines.
It is a beautiful world, snowed-in!

2

Sins were barely noticeable—
Some perversities perhaps,
A slight subtraction of love.
Nothing showed. People
Went to church as usual.

3

Yet attitudes changed. Someone
Had imagination,
Forgot to remember. Elation
Was affected. A grown-up
Said his prayers out loud.

4

"The cow jumped over the moon!"
We shouted in childhood,
Meaning the *WHOLE HOUSE*—
The yard, the stable, the sky
Even, perfection proclaimed!

5

Bishops and popes all over
Harkened to the noble cry—
Poets gave up clichés,
Preachers repetition.
Facts and fission ended.

6

Nothing was like it. Winter
Fell and all who saw it
Walked on the moon, knew
It wasn't possible and settled
Down: what was, as good.

7

O Brahms lay dying, cancer
In his throat . . . Music
Stops. There was a massacre
In Turkey, a synagogue.
What Else? Dislike?

8

Still, the flowers would bloom
Like crazy, three bags
Of sheep manure spread.
You have to prepare properly.
Horticulture is a sermon.

9

So is linguistics. Study
All possible languages,
Inuit or the scrolls
Of Galilee if you can manage.
Personally, I learned English.

10

Brought myself up on Faulkner
And Edgar Rice Burroughs.
I learned a lot about Mars
And what goes on widely
In Yoknapatawpha County.

11

You never can tell. Yet
Again you can: so the snow
Fell in blankets and flakes,
Never stopping, covering
The roofs exclamatory white.

12

"The dish ran away with the spoon!"
Insouciance and
Possibility, high jinks
And cutlery! So much for joy . . .
Hey diddle diddle!

Two Poems in Opposition *

1

Homage to Antaeus

The boulder the angel sat on can have
Its resurrection, I am after
Sensation most times now
Rather than eternity. I would rather
The barebone boulders—that oversoaring
Mycenaean dome lacking
Agamemnon in it,
The exalted vaulting itself the legend:
Helen beautiful and the whole of Troy
Burnt rafters because of her. I'd rather
Go out and look at the stars burning
To a cinder, unimplicated
Whether God is up there
With his unimpregnatable mother.

> Grass that is grass
> Stone that is stone

Music whose meaning is the sound it creates—
The diver's grace, pagan sun on crystal—
Wisdom to stub my toe on the steps
Of the bridge at the Accademia in Venice;
I look at the scar on my left knee
I dropped on still there from last
July, the joy incorporated.

---

* In Greek mythology, Antaeus was invincible as long as he touched earth.
Heracles overcame him by lifting him from the earth.

2

In Praise of Heracles

Suddenly there was a breath of air—cool
Air, after heat, a fresh
Insistence under the glare of sun,
It was as if a clarity was come,
Decisiveness from the north while the garden
Is in bloom—late May
When the ground-phlox takes over,
White and crimson in every corner
Of slant and rock and the blossom of apple
Out and the harsh bronze of peony
Stalks that foretells the future—a confusion,
Breathless, ill-assorted, of sensation
Wanting the complicity of correction and consequence—
White marble, the Parthenon
Whose ordering is the coolness of thought.

   The ocean alongside
   Is only exultation.

  Uneasiness occurs when over the shoulder
The impossible song of the thrush thrives
And sounds, in some foliage claimed by it.

Stances of Prehistory

1   At Altamira

These great drawings, without evolvement,
Deer, horses, aurochs—
Contours, shapes of the rock made use of—
Mammoths, arrows through them,
Solicitations not to gods
But to brush-stroke, colour, creation,
Prayer to itself.

Handle the torch carefully in these caves!
Lie backward, the living ceiling
Is burnt ochre and brown,
As it happened,
Unappointed.

So Gaudier saw inside his stone
(A sabre-toothed cat),
As Debussy wrote, as he felt,
In major, in minor,
As Milton shaped his
Magnanimous cosmology—

Within these caves Plato exacted contraries,
John of Patmos, revelations.

2   At Les Eyzies

Music then?
In the ice-age, a flute of bone—
Handle the evidence,
Three stops in a bird-bone,
Sound in order, consecutive sound,
The world less without it!
In an overhanging abri, two of them
Together: harmonies,
The breath that Lully late let go,
Papageno's happiness!

Humlet for Walking
in Père Lachaise Cemetery

Waste and nonsense,
The grief
For carnal resurrection.

The loss!

Chopin, Oscar's wit,
Héloïse for Abélard . . .

How Still the Wholly Silent Day Is

How still the wholly silent day is,
The seeming living light never tired of.
The sun sets northerly, the last of summer
On the unchanging hills.

It is a holy hour given over wholly
To itself, no word proposed,
Remembering
Abated for an hour.

When last the sun went down there was quiet
As this hour is quiet,
Summer's margin gone,
The sky uncertain now, uncertain.

The Death of Barbara

"We will blow out the sun and the moon.
Ride up the hill of glory," Emily
Wrote. By death only, by death only.
The sentences of life are well drawn—
Death dissembled until the body gives in.

She is dying. While the sun burns
And the moon rides, the end of life
A pretence only.

How easier to accept nothing, no glory.
A stone the better conclusion.

Next Year, It Could Be

Next year, it could be, that the music
Will be heard, phrasings, meanings, carried
Across bar-lines, the exactings,
Declaring what has always been,
Clarity and the calm of knowings,
Acceptances held in the mind and heart
Until accordance is a choice
Natural as the fall of sound
In its virtue understood
As light on crystal is, constant
To the shaping laws; a rooftop cock
Turning round, the wind as it will
Though N points north, the heart responsive.

Sounds

Hoo! Ho! he said, the maker of rhetoric,
Knocked about by cornering winds and waves.
The sound of things is sufficient, the house snapping
In midwinter, the oil-burner clutching
On in the basement, the consignment of pots and pans.
What noise a saw makes makes
A saw. A hammerfest a hammer hammers.
That is the only sensible answer of sense.
How about the morals of a moribund missionary,
You ask? Whatever clatter you want to make
Of a bucket in a well of pure water especially
If a puritan pulls it up. Who needs virtue
Attached to a bird especially if it is scarlet-combed
With a paradise tail? So the winds go
And the waves breaking and nothing lost, hearing
The horizon toss and the moon pull. Standing
And listening you can have everything for a full life
If you want to, the whimper of an animal caught, even,
Let alone of a child.

Ha! Back up. We are back on morals!
To the grabbing ocean and the grass never still . . .

Apparition

deflection of a grassblade,
      a stairstep,
         espousal
   of lip and malice.

Of Minor Matters

They are in their cemeteries, these poets.
Too bad but grief is a candle (burning),
How they got there, their responsibility.
I light out for far places, less able
To sustain indifference, it is true,
Heave baggage up. The white birch
I planted for Johannes Brahms' birthday
Bothers me, whether it is a white birch,
It looks too blotched in the bark to me,
But Paganini's Guarnerius locked up
On its stand in a cupboard in the municipal building in
    Genoa,
Concerns me much more than poets' graves
And domesticities. Irving Berlin could play
The piano only in the key of F-sharp.
That bothers me. But what the Vatican has done
To Michelangelo's ceiling and why the Sacred
College kept Paganini out of his grave
And plagued Galileo is of immediate concern.
Above all, what make of mind would poison
Rivers. This with Muslim hatred of innocence
Has to be rounded up rather than the deaths
Of previous poets and the binding of pristine books.

    I start for Venice and Rome again in July
Despite the exorbitant prices and the heat.

Evidence for the Time Being *

1

Where you sit I study you
the sun across your shoulders
    so strong
        you bend aside,

acceptance, your nature is gentle acceptance

        as though a river flowed,
        a rock marking the timeless flow . . .

        at marble persepolis,
        the horse of dawn
            in the dust of Macedon

        Saint Francis preaching to brother worm

Whatever the circumstances outward

        the liner *Elizabeth*, burned,
        lying on its side in Hong Kong harbour—

        and that uncut ruby for sale in Hong Kong

        the gamelan music,
            in Bali the delicate music

        at Lautoka in the Fijis the trees bent double
            in the hurricane
                and it did not matter

        the ships in English Bay, Vancouver, empty of cargo
        the water not touched they float on

---

* The title for a prose memoir which became "Configurations at Midnight."

2

Projections,
of where repose is

Sun across the sill
lower now

3

And that far local scene

the streets grown up in—
From the Studio (54A Wellington North)
looking across the river of St Francis
the tin steeples
the priests, the unwashed cassock

outdoor iron stairs spiralled
to the upper apartments

the memorial to the war dead on the hill

From Wolfe Street
the river gorge of the Magog
that rushing water
school at the upper park

Alone
and nightjars at dusk at the boy's bedroom window
the poem written

4

in summer
Professor Havard the conductor at the bandstand
        in scarlet and gold

        the brass blowing good and true?
        (O Hemingway)

ice-cream cones (five cents) at the Ladies' Auxiliary
table

in winter
the cardboard caps on the frozen bottles of milk
        from the Pure Milk Company
        the caps raised an inch in the air
                a lick undetected

5

At Canisteo, N.Y.
        the upper meadow
        the long sorry masterpiece written
                ("Summer Symphony")

The depth of an emotion
does not need suffering

6

Granted that you are in health
        consider the grandeur of the earth

the number of horses in a field
of pressed diamonds in the earth
        these are not statistics

7

the afternoon sun going—
roped in
    crampons
    an ice-axe
the peak of the Zugspitze above
the whole of lower Bavaria in the afterglow of the sunset

how to get down in the poor light,
the considerations

8

Working against the indifference
    Beethoven deaf
    Degas blind
    Solomon the pianist
        his hand paralyzed

        of Lampman
it is the same in a post office

9

We are in consequence
    Take the bird that builds a nest
        for eggs
    which rats take over for comfort
    which the tree snake demolishes

Mentionable in a small way
    is James Barker showing off his grandson
        in a horse and two-seater concord
        around Wolfe County
    and the snow-house which he built for him
        that does not melt.

In Cambodia
   for the student of racial power
   a million skulls are displayed

   10

The wind piled in the southeast
   heavy with November rain—
It always comes down the Massawippi Valley
   from Vermont, the North Country

there is no protection no not in heaven
   as long as you are alive

   11

She turns the pages in the history she is reading
   of Athens
      Periclean Athens

Bend down the corner!

Only death can kill you, Mr Bray the grocer said,
   dying of cancer,
      going back to polishing apples

Oh well, Jesus sat on His own tomb

religion assured by Michelangelo's Sistine ceiling

12

The suffering of others is the worst emotion to
endure—
                              whence honesty

Mankind cannot sustain oversight for long

the whole of Midland, Texas, turned out to save a baby
        fallen in an abandoned well.

No one will put up a monument to your diabetes.

                13

Help me, my father pleaded, dying,
                        in an oxygen tent

There must be a better arrangement
                        than drowning in our own lungs.

"What I'm really interested in," said Albert Einstein,
        "is whether God could have made the world in a
                        different way."

Some recommend faith their eyes on the crucifixion
                        worse
                                but quicker.

                14

Over the calm ocean the outward eye is drawn
the slow tide pulling the heart into acceptance
                        the earth leaned on its axis

                already in the evening
                        the snow falls

15

Sorrow admitted and not accepted
remembrance not an exacerbation

At her desk in the alcove
                        night now
        the lamp turned on

16

So it is, so it is

1992

CONFIGURATIONS
AT MIDNIGHT

To have gathered from the air a live tradition
— EZRA POUND, *Canto LXXXI*

A fury for indulgence
— WALLACE STEVENS, *Letters*

Foreword

The usual method for memoirs is prose. Poetry ensures the least fabrication.

I had no wish to proceed by unrolling the epiphanies of a soul from prelude to revelation. An irreverent sense of irony and comedy dissuades me. But I have, strongly, as all creation has, a rage for order. The Greeks looked at their stars and put them into configurations. So have I mine.

I continue the poetic method of contrasts and counterpoint I used in a book called *Gradations of Grandeur*—the affirmation of life through a sequence of poems expressing the fragmentation and disbeliefs of our times, and the resolution which is joy. The procedure accommodates contemporary experience, the speedily moving mental and emotional succession, the historical and private intrusions inherent in our existence which excite immediacy. With poetry which denies disorder, coherence is not lost.

The level of communication that is current was a problem.

R.G.

North Hatley
1992

Index to Configurations

Prologue

So, to match the moment making
    Death a heraldry
Of which there is no claim,
    The heart and mind brought
Into one so that the sun
    On the day that is,
        Is forever had—
    The foliage of a garden,
        A frond, a flower,
    A happening of importance,
Within the house, a room,
    A glance of glass, a going,
A graduation so compelling
    Dimension is not thought of
    Nor death brought in.

So, I seek the world,
    A renewal of moments:
The far reaches of the world
    A happening, a stance,
    A music elsewhere heard,
        Each a wisdom:
The ruined temple abandoned of gods;
Three awkward saints on a brick wall
    (*Bassorilievo* sec. X-XI)
    As at Bologna that day,
Jesus and his cohorts, Vitale and Agricola,
Three little men carved by devotion,
    Twice now to seek them out;
The market-street in Paris that summer,
    She who sold potatoes,
        Red strawberries,
    Who smiled in recognition
    Though a winter had passed—
All allegations compounded of memory,
    Life's renewal.

Mohammed's footmark in rock,
Rameses' lights in a Canopic jar,
        The Valley dust;
Under a lid in Lachaise,
        Oscar's wit,
The music's theme *da capo*.

        The repetition,
        Hurt ignored:
The little girl, cross-eyed,
Hearing herself a "four-eyed bully,"
Crushing her glasses underfoot—
        The one,
October leaves in the garden,
Who now plants bulbs to have
        Spring's yellow
        Who knew hurt.

        It is possible:
        Spring's announcements,
            Love.

Death?
There is no answer.
Jacob climbs his ladders,
Simon quits fishing,
Martha's fishpot waiting on the stove,
God come down, so made flesh.
Buddha's suppliants write hope down
On bits of paper tied to the temple's bush—
Balaam's ass stubborn to stick and pull.

Renoir arthritic, tied his paint-brush to his wrist . . .

    On slack pillows,
    Jaw fallen open,
      We smell.

   The flesh is sensitive.

It is supposed to be sufficient
To stand in the dark of Chartres cathedral
Under the stained-glass windows,
The sun flooding in. I have also sat
Nine times in Bayreuth's *festspielhaus*
Four nights together listening
To Wagner's myths. Faith is complex.

On the far side of the table Peter and Thomas
And the others took bread from the board and brake it
And swallowed a bit of wine.

So we lean this way and that on the moment
(The moment assumed to be the way we want it).
Church bells ring in godless Moscow. The Berlin wall
Is down. Desire in grace is epiphany:
Where the meaning is: the August sun
Ripens a field of standing wheat, a horse
Rubs its behind on a beechwood tree.

Being is what the instructed heart has.

Renewal—that reach of ocean, that span of land
Ancestral to the pole, how many times the conviction!
I keep a stone of the Parthenon on a bedroom shelf,
A painted stone of Altamira as if Rembrandt's hand
Were in it; a feather a swan of Avon dropped
(That day in love, she in the yellow-green dress),
Displayed, velvet Arlecchino from Venice next to it
Leaning against the wall in lightweight socks—
No buskin, the comedy not yet over.

    The future:
    The mind as it is

       ֍

One future can be dismissed:
That it was all foreseen and therefore wanted.
Not by a long shot! the future
Planned and ordered and called our past?
Namely, what was, justified?
Perpetration let off?
Call up the sorrows of the world!

So?

    Free-will. That's the So.
    Job is no answer, wimp
    On an ash-heap with boils.

   It's blustering outdoors. I raise
   The collar of my coat and fit in.

Eaves run wild.
The brook is wild.
On a slant leaf
Accumulation . . .

I go to Washington, Sunday,
To see the cherry-blossoms.
The daffodils already over their peak.

In the National Gallery
Artists have been fixing the world,
Cézanne's Still Life of an apple,
Zubaran's saints.

The attendance, my nose tells me,
      Seldom wash.
   The image of God.
     (I guess).

    (I too prefer art.)

   (But not free-will over people.)

    (Soap over steeple.)

⁙

Just to have her walk into a room
Downs decadence. It is so.
What Alexander burned at Persepolis
From a surfeit of wine and passion was empire.
I have love.

Look!
The racoon rests in the fork of a tree.
I have seen her teach her cubs to open
The trash can, clamp locked over,
Hung on the telephone pole against
The possibility. No Alexander needed.
The good smell got to her. The inner
Side of the tomb of Edward the Confessor
In Westminster Abbey once had a hole.
A choirboy put his hand in
And drew out the Confessor's cross.
Many pilgrims sought the miracle.
I feel secure about her walking
Into a room. The lilies are clothed.

> One might mention the wet of water
> Where the stream flows;
> The sunfall, then dawn over the hills.

> Water for Jesus to walk on.

Yeats for his comfort rebuilt a tower
To live in at Ballylee in Ireland,
Great beams and three-inch planks
To support his inspiration, miraculous
Water wasn't at hand. The house
I chose is two levels above
Lake Massawippi with a hedge and tree
Planted forty years ago
For words and silence. Frost had a farm,
Voltaire a garden, Byron nowhere.
Love, the place the effect is,
We choose early. Keats held
His brother dying, Romeo
Drank poison, believing love.

Charles Chaplin walked tightropes,
His binoculars backward in the circus.

๛

I have seen much.
I have never seen
The file of ants
Walking up
A fencepost,
Each carrying
A white petal,
But I hope to.

The taxi-driver I took on Santorin—
The half-exploded island in the Aegean Sea—
Atlantis sunk with all its perfection beneath
The wine-dark sea—the polaroid of him
I took fixed on his windshield fading in the sun,
Not a time he passed but he put both hands
Out the driver's window and yelled "Xairete!"
"Rejoice!"

The Greeks have a word for it: life!
Permission! whether Hamlet sit and mope
Or Saturn with his fool's crown on, laugh
Bent over and hold his sides.

                    The world
is beautiful. Breakers break
Upon the sands, Orion
Brilliant across the west.
     We watched the Pleiades of August,
Showers of stars fell that night,
Magnanimous rejoicings
Over Cavendish Beach . . .

North where I live the crocus blooms
For about four weeks, less,
Perhaps, I haven't counted, being
Too busy with coming peonies,
Then July green peas,
Then August Indian corn
(Eight minutes under is all you need,
The water already boiling)—
Far quicker than reading
Remembrance of Things Past.
George Eliot's *Middlemarch*
Matches eating corn though
And Chopin's "Barcarolle," peas.

Man shall not live by cake alone.

          All her life that cripple
          Prayed on her kees, the rose-window
          Of the cathedral behind her.
          Biogenetic surgery, I am told,
          Will help, in time.

My father liked fish more than
Answers. He had an answer,
A day in a rowboat, in the sun, fishing,
Pipe lighted, moving the boat
Every once in a while with an oar
Into the shade where the fish are hungry.
I go to Westminster Abbey
And look at Henry the VII's ceiling.
He fished. Ichthus and creation!
Not much to choose between . . .
The context has lost out: London
Is no good, indifference is moved in,
Oxford Street and superiority
Of cultures, cigarette ends.

Keats and his steadfast star, Sterne with his rage,
Dying.

        Conditional joy. That's about it.

        Artur Schnabel gave a piano
        Recital at Oxford in 1930
        At the Town Hall. The Hall is to the side
        Of Great Tom, the five-ton bell
        Of Christ Church College that strikes
        101 strokes each night
        At five-past-nine to toll
        The original number of Fellows in.
        He was in the middle of Beethoven's
        Opus 106, *Die Grosse*
        Sonate für das Hammer-klavier.
        His wont was to play all four
        Of the last sonatas of Beethoven
        At one sitting. Impressionable.
        He entered the *Adagio sostenuto*
        Appassionate e con molto

Sentimento, the third movement
Of the *Hammer-klavier*, when Great Tom struck.
He pulled up. Nine. At the bong of twenty,
Left, the *Fuga a Tre Voci*,
Con alcune license, nobility,
Passion, expressivity, all,
All but the untimely tolling lost.

> Greatness finished,
> Completion lost.

The grinder turns the gilded wheel at the side
Of the calliope on the corner of the Amsterdam
Intersection. We jump out of our skins!
The whole of the Netherlands leaps out of the sea,
The bellows blow heaven up, plug the polders,
Demisemiquavers and accidentals
Sprinkle the air! Out of the silver and ivory
Mouths of the pipes vast processions come!
I drop a gulden in the upturned cap, Rembrandt,
Vermeer, forgotten. Charon grinds away.

> Theme without variation.
> Enter God.

He has a white beard and looks sad.
He wears a nightshirt and is an old man.
He explains everything when you kneel down.
His picture hangs over my crib in a frame.

> It's as good as any.

☙

No doubt of it, dimension is various.
Of Pound's Cantos, scholars will be writing
The poem for him in the thirtieth century
If the treadmill doesn't break down, faculty
Salaries cut, no one to go
To the symposia. Too bad. Pound's
Sea-surge unannotated—
But that's what happens, polymaths
Insisting knowledge is knowledge . . .

        "Wild Strawberries"? Yes,
        I remember Ingmar Bergman's
        Film: the professor emeritus
        Who knew nothing. Yes,
        I remember: he asked forgiveness.

                It's dilation that is in.
                Et alors! Jean sans terre
                Fed his children, *n'est-ce pas?*
                What's fortitude for, more or less?
                Anonymity is his name.

The short of it is known in music as *staccato.*
    In piano performance Rachmaninoff
        Is master of the long of it.
Prokofiev loved the percussive mode. We love it
        To distraction.
We will have to learn *legato* and *portamento,*
        Grace and continuity
                Are out.
Phrasing across bar-lines (not to be disparaged
    Or ignored lightly) and love
                Uncompensated
Are thought boring, years of practice are needed.
        What we do is perfection.

Caliph al-Mansur of Cordoba never rode
Into battle without forty poets at his side—
A love of enlightenment not equalled in the annals
                                        of man—
10th-century southern Spain more glorious
Than barbaric Europe; baths, mosques,
Thirty-five tons of mosaics blue and gold for one
Mihrab alone to pray in, art unparalleled.
    One hopes the poets behaved abnormally
Without back-biting and with craft and humility.

          I think of McDonald's in the eternal city
          A few steps east of the Spanish steps.

The beautiful five hundred and fifty-five times?
Domenico Scarlatti did it three centuries
Ago, sonatas as spontaneous as the word of God.
Bonnington had no time, Rubens a thousand
Overweight dames, Modigliani,
None, Chatterton lying beneath his window's sill
The vial of poison on the floor. Who knows?
A multitude poets write and not a poem;
Vincent cuts off his ear. Disproportion's
Inscrutable—from here to Carnac's runic stones.

          Henry James died of a simple
          Declarative sentence, Schönberg, Mahler,
          Of an attempt at wit. Pollock, confronting
          A perfect cube. No telling.

Life is vagrant.
40% of condoms leak.
The elephant is doomed.
Five children a minute
Are born in Iran.
I try to get through
The tourists in front of
The Bridge of Sighs.

Consider the 2nd edition of the *Oxford Dictionary*,
200 philologists worked for 12 years
Refining the language with timely usages,
Junk food and *born-again* included.

The 27th army moved in
On Tiananmen Square from Changan
Avenue, the Avenue of Eternal Peace,
Wang Wellin calmly stepping
Again and again in the path of the wavering
Line of tanks to stop them. No
Good, of course, as much use
As the styrofoam statue of Democracy
Erected by the students. However,
Comfort can be found. The Sistine
Chapel ceiling is brightened up,
Expert removers are planning to remove
The loincloths on the Last Judgment.
Dimension marches on.

Longevity, shortevity,
Domenico is right:
"Show yourself more
Human than critical," he says.
"Your pleasure will increase . . .
Live happily," he tells us.

Collisions and perturbations nonetheless!
Atomic particles hold their own,
Quantum stability demonstrably works,
The rose is a rose up each spring!
Though fish grew feathers, each is each—
Chattering mankind has his thumb,
Dolphin to dolphin sings. Flamboyant
Nature whose meaning is more than fact,
Profusion piled from pole to pole!
I, lucky Simon, sell my wares,
Study stabilities where they are.

Under what Guidance this lily comes
To fruition is not easily
Found out.

I walk churches guardedly, read
Headstones. I am told
Rest in peace.

There is a paschal bent to the head
Of this lily, a weight to the side
Of Unreason,

Repose so happily biased you conclude
Godwork necessary to account
For the declension.

I study this phenomenon.
Absoluteness pulls me
Unwilling in.

That wasn't what I proposed. For no
Religious reason or faith,
I go along.

Acceptance. That's it. My mind adjusts
To harmony. I make out beauty
And the weight of dust.

There is a duck moving against the stream,
    Excesses of water dripping from its neck.
    Grasses move to the flow of the stream.
        From its hideout below the bank
Surface ripples indicate movement.
    The sun is high, the duck cuts into
    The shade along the north side.
        Noon is gone.

Earlier I had heard the factory whistle upstream
    Where the solitary worker passed
    Carrying his jacket and lunch-pail.
        I was reminded of the lilies
Of the field that toil not neither do they spin,
    The birds clothed and the meek like Solomon
    In all his glory, the earth theirs.
        I am on guard.

The duck is standing on its head in the water.
    Its reach doesn't extend to the bottom
    Unlike the swan's that always seems to,
        Nor do ducks sing.
I watch the duck struggling upstream. Strange,
    The tail is shaking beauty as
    The man with the lunch-pail walks
        Into the distance.

"Supreme fictions" knock one another in my brains,
Earthen pots are earthen pots, the cactus
In them cactus, not fleur-de-lis.
Poetry is what things say they are
However it is thought they aren't. Delicately
Spurred and trumpeted nasturtiums are pansies never,
They are pine-smelling, falling wanly yellow
Before the upper blossoms have scarcely come
White and inconstant red in window-boxes
Where they stand below cottage green shutters.
In the heavenly sense of course everything is fiction.

    All is itself in the quiet light,
       Acceptance inheres,
    Nothing by itself is apart,
       All is one.

    Hills wake to the morning sun
       As dark withdraws.
    The planes of the crystal transact their own,
       All is colour.

    Change to the distant west is come,
       Evening falls,
    There is no ending. Ocean
       Commands no arrogance.

The quiet of this room invites conclusion.
Just now I cut phlox, the pair of rusted
Scissors lost in the garden found again.
I have colour indoors, answer questions.

That same summer at Ogunquit Beach
We were walking around the Marginal Way.

A rainbow fell to pieces above the rocks,
Tumbling red, lessening green—

Of insignificance to navigator Noah
Now that his Ark was steady and the anchor out,

Less to us who still haul up Simon's
Elusive catch, ocean's improvidence.

The impermanence of rainbows, not only along
The Maine coast, is frequent. But still it was pretty.

My neighbour at the Norseman Inn,
A great talker, explains it all.
"Who started the Big Bang?" he says.
God, that's who. Is your beer
Cold enough?" He just might have something.

The blue sky above, a crescent
Of white cloud a closure round,
On the balcony, in her day-book
She quietly writes what has been.

The light was right, the breakers smashing in,
To hold the glorious moment, getting her
In focus, I backed into turmoil.

And so, each year,
The return home.

Love is the answer.
   I watch her,
   By herself,
Raking the grass, the garden's lawn.
   I do not know how to give enough,
      Not adequately,
   So that aware of love's taking
      She has not less.

   I am silent
   So that the cut grass thus
      Be raked aside.

☙❧

Redemption and Destiny both, a wealth!
Chopin's twenty-four Preludes all we need,
Except that note at the end, that D, that D!

Great bursting balls of fire over Venice!
Over Salute; the broad lagoon—*Redentore,*
Redemption, for all the sins of the world!
Cascades pale green, vertical showers
Red, pinwheels, plumes, falling fountains
Of hope, ascendent crimson inside arcs
Of gold inside spirals, silver, shot
With more silver! The houses out in boats
And barges, O more than any Man though perfect
Could redeem a thousand times, more
Than He, hanging high, reckoned for,
Mamma afloat under Chinese lanterns, trestles
Set with checkered cloth and wine and bread,
Yelling kids and fireworks in heaven!

As we sat at the edge of Salute's marble steps,
Lights from the Piazzetta quickened across
The Canal. Grandeur is for a little while.
Our hands together tightened, without fear,
In assertion, the reflection of the lights folding,
                                        shattering.

        Robert Ford. What assertion
        Saved this man, a lifetime dying,
        Standing, helped to stand, unable
        To stand, atrophy, no fault
        His own. What designated regimen?
        Dignity, abrasion, faith? In despite,
        Diplomat for forty years,
        Thereza beside you. That drive uptown
        The four of us in New York City
        Landing the wrong end of Washington Bridge
        Instead of my place for dinner—
        You and Thereza returned to Moscow;
        We in Canada; my answering the Russian
        Ambassador in Ottawa asking where
        Did we want to go? Of all destinations
        My answering Samarkand, destiny
        Made romantic if ever it was,
        Tamburlaine's tomb of jade and those Schools,
        Who piled up death a heap of skulls!
        You in Moscow handling Brezhnev,
        Thereza's ebullence handling the moles,
        A KGB in the front seat
        As we drove to the Bolshoi ballet: "Putting
        Up a statue to the original mole!"

She said in disgust as we passed the Square
On the way to the theatre. "Pink champagne!"
As we sat at the table at intermission.
How did you manage the diplomacy, Robert?
Destiny! Well, retirement to France,
Thereza gone . . . the New York encounters
Gone. Yet the three of us together
At the Chateau Poivrière those days
Before you moved from the empty house—
The back of you in the motor-chair,
Betty walking at its side
Down the roadway as I watched,
The fields, the sky, as if permanent!
And talking poetry that courtyard hour,
Of Canada, Ottawa in error,
You wondering how you'd come this far . . .
Never victim to yourself,
Still we write, the Atlantic between,
Poetry and courage the same thing,
Time and assertion always one.

❦

The heart understands more fully when the body is still.
Space is exhilaration with motion known.
At rest, time forecloses, meaning is.

I have watched a mother watch her child walk
Four steps not moving from her place.

Augustine went aside to pray. The apple
Eaten, Adam begat sermons; sermons,
History down to conclusions. Moses, following
His climb up Sinai soaked his feet
In comforting water. Paderewski demanding
Quiet from the greenroom to the stage, distracted,
                                        went back,
Started over again. Stillness—without
Which, God's inattention. The person
On business from Porlock knocking on Coleridge's door,
Destroyed all Xanadu.

                    No anthems, please.

                    To refresh his soul, Brahms
                    Went to lakes and mountains.
                    Oompah the band played
                    At the Thun village lakeside,
                    His contented beard overflowing
                    So that he did not have to wear
                    A necktie. Occasionally
                    He raised his hat to the evening
                    Ladies he knew in Vienna.

If there are two hundred in the chorus
And one hundred and forty instruments
In the orchestra with eight Wagnerian harps,
                    The music is better?

A complex business this being here, the astonishment
Of walking a planet, a harsh birth and subsequent
History. A godstroke? I search the puzzle of the leftover
Earlobe, the house of the ant, two men
In mortal conflict. I sense haphazard elation.

If one has to make a stand, the end
Is a good beginning. For a start, try
The encompassing fugue at the end of a piece
Of music or if you prefer gardening
Try the trowel on the roots of calendars.

I tried it at the Monastery in Kiev, tried
On for size the skulls of the monks
Underground where they lived to avoid
The soilure and complexity of life by fondling
Heaven. It didn't work. I don't
Care for skulls even when encased
In flesh for viewing. I have better
Means for contemplating heaven.

How to defend oneself against loss is not
By authorization. The walk by Virgin's farm
Upland a mile from here in the chosen evening,
The pasture gate perched on five minutes
Before going on, is wholly lovely
As it is. Ambition is the heart of loss.
Enough diversion is around, faith
Included. Job didn't get much out of
Postponement though it worked pretty well
At Gethsemane. Irony is about.
Willed or not willed as it wasn't, Scott
In his bitter tent fell far short of the Pole.

A brief fall of wet snow,
The sun out again, every
Complex branch glistening, drops
Sharp with accurate colour—
All the eventual story,
Not to be trusted.

At the eastern end of the pillared crypt,
Clothed in scarlet, mitre, gloves,
Lighted by wires and bulbs, Saint Zeno
Lies. The man at the iron grillwork,
Suppliant on his knees, palms
Pressed together, sweats heavily.
A box is nearby for omissions. I walk
The nave. Westerly, the rose-window,
The rounding *Wheel of Fortune* red
And blue about the Virgin, stains
The stone floor. The lower windows
Of shaven amber are forgotten. Sun
Sets the cobwebs on fire.

ༀ

Perfection is hazardous, to be handled
Carefully. Youth is a despoiler;
Age with its establishments.
My father's ebony cane
Had to be put back
Exactly next to the radiator . . .
Symmetry and perfection:
Companions of disenchantment.

From the well out of doors to her house
Mrs. Sibelius lugged
Pails of water. Sibelius
Couldn't compose hearing
Worked pipes and faucets.
Think of his three daughters.
Milton according to his two
Talked like a cathedral.
Mrs Euclid had nightmares.

The razor-blade's in the apple, trick
Or treat; cyanide's in the pill;
The wheelchair's up against the stairwell.
Only comedy will do:
The cops are after Keaton; Hardy's
Down the chimney in another mess,
Laurel shut in the closet so dark
He couldn't hear. If not comedy,
Goodness! Never mind perfection . . .
My mother used to get red in the face
With laughter, the ridiculous was so great.
What was, I never knew.
Sad by nature, she loved to laugh.
Her china cabinet stood in an angle
Of the dining-room, the glass sides
Were curved. How could glass curve?
She laughed that day as though the china's
Rims of painted flowers had blossomed,
As well they might with her near;
Her goodness had wondrous complications.
Happiness today; remembered.

What we need are playpens
For children, pencils on desks
Out of reach of statisticians.
Fire and the wheel again. What
Beginnings are. Poems to say so.

Notwithstanding!
Euphoria is in the air,
The century's done!

The sound was of broken glass. The sentry at the end
Of the Kurfürstendamm looks up. Households
Come out; Leipzig jams its streets; a hundred
And fifty thousand lighted candles shine.
No one packs a gun. Doorways are jubilant.
The file-room's inside out, papers blow.
A bicyclist rides the Berlin wall, a gentleman
Chisels loose a brick. Rumania's flag
Has a hole. The Pope speaks in thirty
Tongues. Networks prophesy. The shed
At checkpoint Charlie's carted somewhere else,
The janitor in it. Cloisters abandon prayer.

In Canada for three days there was wind and snow,
Parliament commended caution; in protest, females
Marched; remarks were made in Senate. The Bay
Lost money, burglars struck. The Coaticook bank
Bilingually posted notice: "Fermé. Hold up."
Hockey prevailed.

Not yet Becket's dustbin,
Humanity dumped.

O "theory of everything!"
"Subnuclear zoo!"

I stand by the window. Nothing
Is more at one than this day
Deliberately chosen, the exactions of winter
Everywhere, marks in the snow,
Twigs drop blizzards, the squirrels sitting
Appleboughs nibbling wizened
Apples left hanging by sloppy November.
I turn away, my consciousness imposing
What it would, still it comes—
The black-rimmed stationery message.
Now it's McDonagh, maker of handsome
Books as if there was no end.

Tonality, tonality lost, Liszt's
"Die Trauergondel," that damned carriage
Off to San Michele, the double
Oars not interrupted,
Resolution none . . .

It cut like crimson across the west—
The sun, thought of as of no consequence.
I shut my eyes, close off sight.
The slash on the inner dark is there,
The slash, cut across all augury.

Methane to oxygen to the first fish, this dappled
Sapphire, earth, grabbed excuse,

Continuum in perpetuum, ignored elegy,
Apprehending. The grass is green,

At times we love one another! Departure
To all the dead well dead!

Who'd skip the gridlock? Scrape
Two sticks together—a blinding light!

I breathe, scent air, against all brokerage,
Sometimes, right urgencies.

    The promise of evening is kept, the weather
    Sullen, but newness of birds, ten
    Hours survived.

    Tomorrow could be accepted, protests
    Democratically posted, documents
    Launched and rescinded.

    Dawn's daring stretching, birds
    Singing all over again. I too
    Tire easily—

    But a presence of stars is everything,
    Perhaps enough even the moment
    Of sorrow come to.

We walked through the golden mist, the gate that we
                                  knew—
Monet would have painted the light—

The great doorway to the house of Agamemnon,
Of Clytemnestra, the amorous pair

Loved by death. We walked in richness, she,
I, through the Lion Gate, careless

Whether Paris went to bed with Helen
Or not, the morning of more importance

Than Mycenae ruined, Rouen painted—the Argive
Fields heavy with a second year's barley

More golden than the dead king's flattened mask.
The sun was out as we had ordered it—

A thousand Troys burning crazily at the other
End of the Mediterranean celebrant,

History on the crumbling Herculean
Walls at Tiryns nothing to our richness.

She counts the number of buds on the impatiens plant
There on the coffee table. The eaves
Outside have snow.

The set of painted angels and donkeys with Joseph
And the wise men around Mary
Holding her wooden Jesus

Bought in Copenhagen, are in place on the mantel.
A risen star is over the verandah.
In fact, hosts of them.

This is the third December she has trimmed the impatiens
She tests the soil and with the green watering-can
Has blossoms all winter.

We were above the clouds.
No one could have ordered a more beautiful
Floor of heaven, gold,
Unstable gold to the horizon.
An adorable child kicked
The back of my seat, food
Came locked in plastic,
The tray was down. The man
Adjacent talked for himself.
I managed to uncross my legs.
I had to go. Trolleys
Clogged the aisle. The restrooms
Were full. My heart was full.

The five-day ocean passage spent on the boat
Named after her of the cockeyed hats, the Mary of The
Royal line, preserve those boats set
To the rusted glory of wasted time! Leg-room,
Sea-air, promenades and privacy! The bingo
Purser's gambling "shake the bag," midnight
Won! Behrman's wit, Coward's puns!

Apart from housebroken children
The present race is not worth it. Barely.

She goes into the history of diapers
As we ate; dropped the used
Huggies later in the waste-basket
In my study. My theory's correct.

I look for the *concierge compatissant*;
The *cassiere* who can add.
Once eating Nuremberg bratwurst
At the café behind the cathedral in Munich,
The Bavarian opposite asking for the garnish
Said "Danke." Unheard of in Canada.
And sample England's London now
The Commonwealth is there . . .

Jonathan Swift preferred horses,
Loved Tom, Dick and Harry.

⚘

Attacked by a crocodile
In the jungles of Mato Grosso,
You my resourceful composer,
Heitor Villa-Lobos,
What did you do? You stuck
A stick upright in the gaping
Jaws and saved yourself
And Brazilian music, that's
What you did, fabulator
Of ten-foot stories. How
The critical cognoscenti
Swallowed your crocodile whole,
Lover of Bach and a large
Cigar (which you light) wearing
My coat with the beaver collar,
Canadian and mestizo out
In the snows of wild Connecticut!

You still take that little
Train of the Caipira in heaven,
Steam out this side,
That, whistle blowing
Saudades, the sadness
At the heart of things ever
In your music, rhythm
Going until the heartbeat,
Valves, wheeze and champ,
Wheel flattened, comes
To a stop? I miss you;
Still conduct your music
Silently as you wished!
Adeus, charlatan
In all that doesn't matter,
Lover of "trips around
The world" and such circuits.

The body of poor old Laurence Sterne
Was dug from the graveyard of St. George's,
Hanover Square, by body snatchers.
An acquaintance recognized his corpse
On the dissecting table. What matter?
Who will forget the making of Tristram
When the goodwife asked at his father's
Most salient moment, *Pray, my dear,*
Have you not forgot to wind up the clock?
And little Shandy's circumcision
When the sash of the window fell down?
And Uncle Toby and the whole of the book
Back-end-to? What possible preservative
Halo can fit the immortal head of him?

Somerset Maugham fidgeted in his bath.
"I will not stutter today. I will not stutter
Today," he repeated, then read Voltaire and Milton
To tune his mind for his morning's limit of prose,
The top hat and ascot necktie worn
To displace his stutter, kept to celebrate
His wife's funeral. Something of an "old
Chinese madam in a brothel," summary of the portrait
Sutherland later painted, stuck to him,
Hence the apparel, three fashionable hits
In the West End theatres at one time.
The ugly Villa Mauresque he had at Antibes,
A foible. From the table, we climbed to the top of the house,
The brick-walled room, the one window
At his back so he could write free of the beauty
Of the Mediterranean. He knew what is but couldn't
Have it, died rich, first of the second
Rate, friendly—if it didn't interfere.
Loved little, Vuillard and "Born Yesterday."

    That great booming voice—
    Paul Robeson in concert—
    Larry Brown accompanist
    Chiming in once
    In a while—*Joshua fit*
    The battle of Jericho,
    Oh, yez, *and the walls*
    Came tumbling down
    Except that we had to sit
    Upstairs on the balcony
    In the Ivy Restaurant
    Of London that night
    Because you were black. We did.

And we went into Surrey—Bramley—
And the four of us played cards,
The cows mooing outside
And the scenery all countryside,
Remote and undirecting
Except to loveliness,
And you slammed down hearts
Like crazy unleashed taking
Tricks and we forgot
That the moon sets, thought it
Still climbed eastward
Where the haystack was and you
Predicted literary
Immortality for me,
And I, that the last two stones
Of Jericho finally
Hit the dust and Ajalon
And Goshen and all the land
Even unto the land
Of Gaza came out in brilliant
Stripes and polka dots
And there was no midnight ever.
How's that, Paul?

And you, sculptor of clay
And stone, Jacob, never
Sir Jacob Epstein thou wert!
You were too natural for that,
Your hands in granite dust
And the reluctant earth, yet
Honour had to invest you.

You saw Lucifer and Adam
Naked (a shilling a look
In a Blackpool basement;
At Père Lachaise graveyard
Your Oscar Wilde memorial
Covered by French authorities
With a tarpaulin—the penis
Broken off for a keepsake).
"Hats on, Gustafson!"
You said that day we went
By taxi to Cavendish Square
Together taking a good look
Up at your Mary and little
Boy over the arch of the Convent—
Never so tender a Mother
And Child cast by anyone,
Verrocchio or after.
And Kathleen (quoting Dante)
At the Isola Bella restaurant
In Frith Street and the one
Behind the Ritz Hotel,
Pointing out models for you!
And your Queen's Gate studio—
The children's heads in plaster
All over the frontroom piano,
Loved and immortal bubbles,
African masks upstairs
Before Picasso thought of them,
Churchill in residence across
The street, you, honest,
Hating all critics.
Mazel tov, Jacob,
Of elemental power
You never thought of!

"Poetic freedom within a basic
Pulse." Shadows murmur in the street,
The evening gone. Exact measure
In spontaneous grace. Those who last,
Have it: Hopkins; Ezra, some,
All freedom, nowhere to stand.
Browning has it. Jazzmen and horses
Sometimes, sewers of silk.
Not the world theirs but what they do,
Symmetry, fury, out of love.

∽

Near Bronzolo north of Verona from Munich,
Clouds dark and pierced lay across
The contour of the mountains, the valley below heavy
With vines rich for harvest, the rows thick,
Hardly breathing left for the gatherers between.
The village spire pointed to God, lover,
We are told, of men, the pastor at hand, portly,
Rich of voice loving the tale good
To hear many times. How they laid
The wire along the pylons, chasms between,
Impossible to tell, but always the way home
Still to be found by the light of the windows on
At night—a fable the pastor, down to earth
Like God on high, did not forget.

The sun
Usually burned off the broken cloud
By late morning, marble strata left showing
Too out of the way for easy quarrying.
Riches are the province of heaven, the pastor made known.

I dreamed white whales,
Evil swam the seas.
A black sun was up.
Armour moved: treads
And crushings; mindless hate.
Contempt spat in the food.
Iron crosses burned.
Each thought he was more.
I awoke. I got up.
I brushed my teeth, swearing
The confidence of heaven.

In the Bargello we climbed the stairway to the upper floor.
Saint George was there, little David oh my!
And the baptist shrunk from fasting—David again,
Goliath dripping out his severed neck.
Citizens walked about chewing gum.
Grace outlasts us. Downstairs, Mercury stood
On the wind on one toe; Ugolino,
Starved, and Perseus flaunting his head. I look
For confidence—take heaven at its word.

I must look into
This when dead:
Gulls fit ocean,
Ocean, shores;
The hair the head.
Hollyhock-pods
Shattered in October
Have white and red
At the window in August.
Flesh fits sharks.
Men, God?

෨෬

Creation can't be trusted.
Nature should fit the talent—
Schwarzenegger, brainy;
Rachmaninoff, handsome—
Creative talent, nature;
Dürer put a navel on his Adam.

God knows what man disposes!
Picasso's women have two noses.

Adam and Eve in the thirteenth century mosaics overhead
In the southerly porch of St Mark's cathedral in Venice
Fidget uncomfortably in their first clothes.

Rubens' overweight dames furtively
Fondled as he painted them fill wall after wall
Of the Alte Pinakothek museum in Munich.

Authors should fit what they say. Samuel Beckett
Walking in the park on a sunny London day,
His companion remarking the day made one glad
To be alive, answered, "I wouldn't go that far."
His creation, Murphy, dreaming his life away
In a rocking chair, blown to bits when
The gas-plant explodes and shreds him, directed
His ashes be flushed down the toilet of Dublin's
Abbey Theatre. Utterly committed to despair,
Beckett wrote on fervently rescuing his future.

"Endgame"
Puts mankind
In an ashcan.
The text is revised
With great care.

I am listening to a Sonata for Flute and Cembalo
By Bach, arranged for piano by Kempff,
Played by Lipatti. Over lucid?

Poor Seyfried, invited by Beethoven
To turn the pages for him at the first
Hearing of the Third Piano Concerto
(Hearing! The ear-trumpets grew larger!),
"Heaven help us!" Seyfried wrote,
"That was easier said than done.
I saw almost complete blank
Pages at most . . . There were what looked like
A few Egyptian hieroglyphics
Which served to remind him of salient ideas."
Heaven serves the indecipherable.

Books? Unto the utmost! shelves
Of them. Multiplied! One
More and we have to move, the weight
More than we can bear, the depth
More than we can plumb, the longest,
Always going to be read, the shortest,
Never enough. Once, putting
My books in order, I failed to notice
An earthquake (minor). Books are fatal.
To turn the pages of his Book of Hours,
Subtly poisoned, Francis the Second
Of France, licked his finger; the pianist
Alkan, reaching from his library ladder
For the Mishnah on the top shelf,
The bookcase fell on him. "No furniture
As charming as books," says Sydney Smith.
I still intend to read Gibbon.
I keep settling for "Through the Looking-Glass."

Of authors there is no end.
At fifteen I had
Three chapters of my novel,
"Westward Ho with Columbus!",
Done. I got to where
The mutineer dangles
From the yardarm "like a spider
From his web"—a simile
I thought highly of. For proper
Appreciation in Sherbrooke
At the time, there was a visitor
From New York, Miss Catherine Adams,
Author of a book about girlhood.
She was published. My mother,
Experienced, invited her
To tea. She enjoyed it.
She thought my three chapters
"Memorable." Macauley the historian
Has a similar verdict:
"I have read your manuscript
And much like it." Disraeli
Assures an author, he
"Would lose no time reading
His book." I discovered these comments
Later on though.

    "We authors," as Queen Victoria
    Said to Lord Beaconsfield.

☙❦❧

Much is required for an adequate answer:
The cockroach is repulsive and the female
Produces three hundred, four hundred,
Offspring at a time. It hates light.
We may expect that the life-force
(Or Original Light as some put it
Wanting to escape institutional God)
Is not entirely related to Purpose.
How equate the cockroach
With single-minded Benevolence? Dichotomy
Infests the world. Some predict
The cockroach like the Biblical frog
And locust will take over the earth.
The scent of the dog, the reach of the giraffe
And the wings of the hummingbird, of these
There is no need of further praise.
I am halted by the cockroach and innocence.

I was ashamed killing the spider.
The deed was inadvertent. I was laying
The log on the fireplace when frenzied
By the heat he came out from under the bark
Of the birch and scampered into the flame.
Gone.
    Life's surgence is sacred.
Participants of supposed perfection,
This one religiously burns opponents,
This one attends cecal cancer.
I see no subtlety but to accept:
Leave entrails and flame up to Him
And sort the categories out.
I study the cobweb intricate in the sun
And a slight wind and I am perplexed,
Shamed for no human reason.

In one day the floodwaters rose
Covering the fields each side of the road.
Cattle drowned. Cows were moved
To higher ground, fodder carted.
Snow was heavy all winter
And now melted. Each stone
Stopped spirals of colour, embrasures
Spilled back to green stubbings.
A leg stuck up. Crows came.
Accomplishments of harvest were cancelled.

Life subject to death. I walk along
This cornice of field, easeless, aware of what
Was achieved: a jewelled egg, a belt buckle,
Versailles—hand to the new century
Immovable perfections, smokestacks, AIDS,
Equations to settle questions of faith.

The uses of detraction are a Bible
Diminished, the worm knotted in the sun
That thrives, that duplicates buried,
Limbless, eats dust. Izaak
Walton threaded one on the hook
Of his fish line, pulled out Eden.

The beauty of the world is not over.
Unexpected, overnight,
Snow came. An hour and the world
Was white, along the branches thick,
Along the fence, under a moon
The path to the roadway—the cat,
The mole, did not venture out,
No mark until the sun should come—
White to the farthest recesses, man
Himself could not refuse the abrogation;
Accuracy is thought of, the possible
Truth behind the breath of his words,
Of the fall of an interval of music bringing
Resolution. This night of snow, one night
And the heart is itself in exactness.

     Louis Dudek, poet, and I
     Had turned down the Niger River ravine
     Near his house in Way's Mills.
     We had a discussion to settle: why
     God? and if He wasn't would
     We have to have Him? We decided we had to,
     We couldn't discuss God if He wasn't
     And walk down the gulch of the Niger
     In broken dappled sun and approach
     An adequate conclusion. I lost a glove
     During the discussion. The left glove.
     What to do with the right was what
     The walk in the dappled sun came down to:
     Find a perfectly lost left-hand glove to go with
     The right in the time that we had.

Farewell to philosophers and reason,
The mind fumbles, alternates give way.

The cobweb, the crystal of snow, the chameleon's eye,
These are consistent. The whorl of a shell,

The eyelash, these are simplicity. Adumbrations
Of dust spoil consistencies.

Contours are, hills are. Whoever
Wants metaphor has likelihood.

The scheme of the potter is true configuration,
The blower of glass, the warmth of the sun

Beyond persuasion. Our very setting out
Was done in sorrow, promulgations

Of the heart are revised in accordance with clarities
Of the night, Orion and his bow.

⚘

The ambiguity of compensation came
From the surgeon who put my pacemaker in.
"I feel fine—except for deterioration,"
I told him with what I thought was wit.
He laid down the stethoscope:
"You have your imagination."

    Ned Adams my friend who had girth
    He was oblivious of and who brought his films
    To my father's studio to be developed,
    Day or night, the sunniest, wore rubbers
    And carried a folded emergency umbrella.

Earlier, the plane ride had nearly
Done me in, a 1926
Open Cockpit Plane it was called,
Privately owned by Bud McRae.
The local runway was at St Hubert
Outside Montreal (saints
Are everywhere in Quebec).
It was twenty-one years since
The Wright brothers. I sat in the rear
Cockpit. Bud stood up on his seat, waved
His arms in the air, both of them. The plane
Dived. My cap tangled in the struts.
I laughed carelessly, the big guy,
Virtuoso.

        The flight (commercial)
Five years later from Oxford to Hanover
Was enclosed. I opened the window's
Slide (the latest advancement) for air
The stream put my antrum back
Sixty years. However, I just
Skipped the voyage the *Andrea Doria*
Sank, the Teheran revolution,
The Thessaloniki earthquake.

I call up the Plymouth Brethren
Funeral of my playmate Ruth
Davis: "It gives me great pleasure
To be here," the minister said.

Mid-August at the Caracalla
Baths in Rome, Tebaldi as Tosca
Could hardly sing. A terrible cold.

I keep promising myself to go to Nepal.
Other people do. Everest,
Nupse, despite the heights. I dare
Destiny, station the Matterhorn
In my window at Zermatt. There it was—
Whymper's ascent. Hudson's shoe
Dug up from the ice, Old Croz
Dead and hapless Hadow. You can have
The Taj Mahal. I have seen the Parthenon.
But Ponce de León's fountain!
I keep on daring, a glass at my elbow
On the slate coping in my garden.

᚛

Diminution's the thing, it chastens
Ambition and suchwise aspirations.
Arranged by Liszt for piano solo,
Dohnányi played for me one day
The "Pilgrims' Chorus" from *Tannhäuser*,
A grapefruit in his right hand—
Teeyum teeyum teeyum in the treble
Down; the black-key *Etude* by Chopin
With a hairbrush, *tum-tum-*
TUM, etc. Who could wish
For more? He was a musician after
My own heart, honoured solemnity
With perspective as Arthur Loesser
Did who gave recitals of the world's
Worst piano music. Caruso
In the midst of *Traviata*
Passed a raw egg to his soprano.
Poor Violetta, it did her
The world of good.

We swam at Smyrna—where the Greek girl
Lived whose son was Homer—in Izmir's
Glass-walled pool. Intricate alleys
Led to Homer's ruined home.
We watched the sun set in gold
Over the Aegean sea, listened,
The lap of Triton's turmoil touching
The edge of Miletus' marble steps.

The longboat's keel strikes the shallows!

Pergamum is grass; Didyma's
Amphitheatre empty: Apollo's
Shadows no longer Persia's pride.

Einstein loved his violin
The equal of any equation.
Playing sonatas with Godowsky
The piano virtuoso,
Einstein lost a measure,
Godowsky his cool. "What's
The matter with you?" cries Popsy,
Slapping the lid of the piano,
"One, two, three,
Four. One, two—
Can't you count?"

I watched Einstein as the honorary Oxford
Degree in latin went over his head.
His eyes twinkled relatively.

"You are one of my heroes,"
I said to Charles Chaplin.
Top that stultifier.

Mr D'Attili
Of Dumont, New Jersey,
Is happy. He sits
In his basement appraising
Violins, violas,
Cellos. He's happy
Just holding them.
As many as possible.
He does not want to be
A millionaire.
Maria his wife
Sifts the requests
From four continents
Made to consult him.

Hucksters, critics, whoever forever
Breaks what he picks up are a part
          (I suppose)
Of this engaging beautiful world and (perhaps)
Are eminently worthy of affection
          (I hug you, O huckster)
Especially if they have only one
Last china plate of that pattern
Dropped from the rinsing pan
          (O Chinese Pan!).
I am not talking of awkwardness
          But of those who don't care
In a world uncaring enough as it is
          (Hear, here, bassoons and tubas!):
Of slobber of deconstruction got rid of nearest at hand,
          (O academics),
Beer-bellies and abandoned hypos
          (The beach was miles),

She who keeps saying "You know"
        (Not till you tell me, dearie)
            (I mean),
The stoned, not the thrown-at,
The gesture and not the commitment,
Batter, not the silence
        (Blesséd be *pianos*),
The spitter, not the spitten
        (O baseball!).
    May all be considerate,
    May all have humility.

    O the unbalance of things:
    The linguist and his super trumpet.
    "He didn't kill nobody, you know . . .
    I was like nineteen or something, man—
    You know, wild. I didn't care."
    He speaks lovely, eh man?
    Blow, Gabriel, blow!

❧

And so it is, there is, no,
There is never enough of equity,
Of walking the measurable earth,
Stones against the impressionable heel,
The inlet, water and soil both,
The pathway along the shore; deep
Snow, reluctant. Moments remain.
Grief, yes. But not those moments
Taken once unnoticed: the two of us
Together on the Acropolis
Taken by the wandering photographer,

Seated on the fallen marble of Athens,
Arrived at happiness; Lake Vänern
Of Sweden, the moon full gold;
The Göta Kanal's three nights . . .
Ivalojoki, the river that side
The Arctic line of Finland's sun,
The sauna's hot stones and madness,
The icy river jumped into . . . Vesuvius'
Stygian crust walked on. Easter
(A thousand years ago!) the dough
For bread risen over the warm
Floor register. Particulars . . .

Each season's gift returns, the furrowed
Earth the need, Egypt's seasons
Wherein the gods reside,

The noria turning, the altar at Abu
Simbel burdened with fruit and sheaves
Taking the striking sun.

Saskatchewan, wheat slanted to the sky's
Horizon; the apples' heavy covert
Easternmost waited for.

Only man out of season
Surpasses this.
Listen,

You will hear the bone snap.

The body was five thousand years old,
Uncorrupted as if asleep yesterday.
He was untouched, no cerement, priestly resin
Or three-lid coffin—he lay there as himself,
About twenty-five.

            The burial room was down
The twenty-rung wood ladder near
The Chephren pyramid—Sharik Farid (his son
Was turning Eliot's "The Waste Land" into Arabic)
Took us down—the excavated chamber
Kept hidden, I suppose, because the parched
Depth preserved the perfect nakedness.

   Behind the partition of glass his eyes were closed
Quietly, the arms folded, his toes perfect,
The sex rested in the groove of his thighs as if
After having love. The penis, Farid told us,
Corrupts first.

          I wanted to call his name.

      This was before we had climbed up
Inside Cheops' vacant pyramid, saw
Hathor with the cow ears
In her temple up the Nile and passed
Akhenaten's city crumbled to dust.

      What shall we say?
I have no pyramid,
Said words
Silence hears?

        ❧

Ecstasy is as the meaning
Of what is,

Not abstract Plato but someone
sawing wood,

Sawing crosscut birchwood
His mind on dust

Drawn up in the air,
The sorting sun.

In the shallows fish
Swam
Indirections.

The current shoved at
Stones
Capped silver,

Pulled attached
Shadows
Immeasurable.

Nor was silence
A stand-in
For summer
Passed,

Thumbed autumn's
Shortness.
The silence
Was love,

Extensions of nothing
That is nothing
Without
That love.

⟊

Circumstances matter.
Matilda Carpenter lived
In Norton Mills, not
So far from Lime Ridge—
Where of all places
I was born. Norton
Mills is in the state of
Vermont where she bore
My mother Gertrude Barker
In the bedroom partly in Stanhope,
Quebec, the two villages
For all purposes one—
The birthright therefore
Is international, Canada
From sea to sea, the U.S.
Top to bottom.

My father came from Växjö
In Småland, Sweden. He got
A job with the Lime Company
Whose superintendent was James
Barker whose daughter he married
For love. He loved quality,

Wore kid gloves to pile
Cordwood and had no use
For his brother August who,
On his way to Vancouver,
Stole his ivory flute
And brass bed. August
Died young. My father
Lived well into his nineties.
Quality, pursued, pays.

With reference to my father
Taking twice the arsenic
He should have, to speed the cure
Of his legs—and to his brother John,
Dynamiter at the lime kilns,
Stuffing the cliff with twice
The dynamite stipulated
To cut his workload
In half while he had lunch,
A cow and the railcar trestle
Down to the pit demolished—
The rumour is Swedes
From Småland Province are stingy.
I had this from a fellow traveller
On the ferry going from Stockholm
To Finland. He said, as well as
Being stingy, Swedes
From Småland Province where
My father and his brother were born
Are mean. He didn't know
My father and John doubled
Life to save time.

Alas, for ignorance.

My sister who was four years older
Didn't much like me tagging
After her when she played. She had
A den behind the lattice trim
Of the back verandah where she pinned up cutouts
Of Hollywood movie stars; she wore
Stick-out false hair-buns
Each side of her head where the ears are.
Girls talked. I was Tarzan
Clinging just barely to the boulder the glacier
Had left across the street. I was
Also John Carter, Warlord of Mars,
Madly in love with Dejah Thoris.
My enemy was Tars Tarkis
Who was green and had four legs.
The exploits are among world literature.

The house screen door slammed behind him
To keep the summer insects out, my father
Stood a moment to get out his pipe, then scratched
The jamb not thinking of the fragile paint bubbles,
The match flaring crimson an instant, the tobacco
Catching, he standing still to protect the puff,
Then going—walking in the evenings down the hill
To the studio. Where it ran into Montcalm Street
The street was named Wolfe until the French put a stop
To that. Except for the sidewalk it wasn't then paved.
In August the sweet corn in the garden back
Of the house was higher than I was—in the middle of a city.
He turned off down Frontenac Street,
His legs not too good, but you did not know it,
Swedish obstinacy, independent of emotion—
He liked emotion well enough when it was not
Made an instruction. He loved a straight-stemmed
Pipe . . . It smelled good. I still have it.

Remembrances that offer us back: the broken
                                        porcelain
Figure mended in the corner china cabinet;
REGULATOR painted in gold letters
Across the glass front of the wall-clock's
Pendulum which I scratched away with a pin . . .
Appearances: the lace she wore; the song-sheet
Yellowed in the attic, the box one day
Dragged out: the marriage announcement,
                                    the shallow silver
Bowl only, of a spoon; between tissues,
The dress folded, the gloves, forgotten . . . lavender . . .
The leather volume of *Best Loved Verse*
The spine broken. Old letters. Hear me.
I am better than all of this, better . . .

☙

Music itself,
A burst of broken light centred
And splayed in a thousand shatterings of coloured
Vision, impressions on impressions—
The whole an incandescence,
I was without questions,
The location a farther room
Of hers, the chair, the orange leather,
Only the reading lamp on the antique
Desk on. Against logic,
The flaring glass of the empty Orrefors
Vase cut in all directions
Refracted as fire. It was surety.
Without compliance. Of no use.
It was light, silence of light,
It was flame.

Let us translate:

Anger, deputy,
boundaries there are until the spirit
unregulated establish what
has already been known:

Dominion of God and Light
that in fragments
is our use.

Abstract thoughts! these in sensation,
music brought down
in substance manifest.

(Scriabin *Sonata* 5)

Equivalents of tiny bells.
Inquiries of truth and time?
Pacings beside the pool,
    Delicate incense
Spilled inadvertently but
The tiny bells among the
Gongs, equivalents! equivalents!
The gods will hear
        will hear . . .

(Debussy "Pagodes")

Dolce:
Walking slowly, compensation beside
a pond? yes, a border walk—
the rippled surface
quickened, crowded coming,
touch!
        Enough! State it!

Dolce come prima:
the water touched.

Overreach, overreach!
Regular pace, ordered insouciance,
kids dancing to tunes, kids down slides
and skipping better keep beat
or whistle through your fingers,
kicking small heels carefree
the balustrade above the Moscow River
comical, slidings and love (a little),
        but keep time!
the future is here, the future comes!

        (Prokofiev *Sonata 8*)

    Re-Harakhty, God
  Of fire and of the sun.
      This:
      More light.

☙❧

"An absence of being," the Greek says of evil.
More! more than a want of sun,
As a shadow is more, is that which is hidden;
My shadow grows longer, dark insistence
Lengthens me, the equivalence of a century
Is as nothing, my breath enough for only
Dreams of no substance, music unheard.
Absence of poetry! Irony in protest:
I shall go out, hang petals up
With the full moon up, crush
Through the substance of snow, exhibit
Being, words salt on the tongue!

I went out to see if the buds had roughened
The lilac bush. The sun, the April
Air, was mild. March was gone,
The year's harsh winter. Yellow
Along the forsythia branches was tense,
Smoke was reported in the woods where
The maple's sap is boiled. The first
Of the crocus was up. There was evidence of later
Primrose. Immortality was ready,
Double white from the lilac bush.
But whether I was too early thus
Going out or if the maple tree's
Scarlet was fallen, wouldn't matter.

What a conclusion, kettle of fish!
Digging in toes against the tide,
Curtains up in the rinsing morning,
Down again and then night!

Walking landscapes won't work.
Fence-sitting helps, breathing
Air is assurance. But calamity let loose
So faith can be armtwisted, whirlwinds,
Nothing can improve. Correctible
Hurt is man's, not undone
By piety, *tu quoque*, or burning
Joan. I got off the top rail
Sorrow deeper for the lovely view.
Defiance, compassionately plugging holes
Left by omissions, only will do.

> Who heard Beethoven's Ninth
> In Berlin that Christmas, heard assurance.
> Promoters sold pieces of the wall,
> Defiant on one side, as mementos.

O what women bitter at heart
Stand at the edge of the barren fields?
Aged women in bitter shawls,
Babushkas tied under the chin.
It is cold. Bending, life spent bending—
Water from the yard, sickness at the bed.
"The horizon here is forever." Bearing,
Bearing can be a bitterness.
Only at the fence the interval, talking . . .
"The hair falls loosely; it was black, raven,
If you will . . . A man from the backcountry passed
Along the road to Yasnaya Polyana . . ."

Philosophy fails, Absolutes.
Only order, "a rage for order,"
Will do, undoctrined anger,
Adam in his petulant garden,
The mud good and the working sun
Good and the body that legislates,
And knowing the house could be straightened with a
                                                    hammer
If he had one, eating apples worth it—
Fish and fowl and cows and orderings,
Bee-lines, Adam could not name them
Fast enough: loins and love.

He settled down: the spider's selection
Of seclusion, the watercourse salmon
Die in, the hive's retrieval,
Questions of actuality: Schubert's
Inspiration, Cézanne's stroke,
The elephant's domesticity?
All is poetry, poetry.

                        ☙

            And human beings
            Living in imposed
            Filth in Rumania.

Repetition! Inexhaustibility!
On the one hand Monet and his serial
Cathedral-front in unsuspected light;
Each spring, discrimination of experience,
The very hunks and adamants of life
Craftiest subjections; on the other, contradiction!

Christian battles
Islam, Islam
Battles Jew.
Muslim bloodies
Rama, Ulster
Batters Pope.

Abolish god.

It's original sin alright, perfection
Out, dishevelment in.

Consider copulation, joy
Unending, the bottom-line of love,
The silly friction accession to heaven.
Guilt assigned to innocence,
Naked babies washed at the door!
    The rounding world is in jeopardy. Sober
Ecstasy, that's what called for, this flesh
Supposedly worn in the cause of heaven.

    It strikes at any moment, life,
    In the midst of choosing; standing humming
    Silently; combining intimacies; minding
    The mind's business; fifty-five miles
    An hour. no miles per hour.

    Of all the vanities there is none
    As breath. North and the frozen darkness,
    The southern rose halfway open
    Beyond compare—this total—
    Incalculable time or Tuesday next—
    None is as breath. "As sparks fly upward,"
    Says the Book. "A little folding

Of the hands to sleep." That day finally
As wished: time to get there
Not long enough, not long enough there.

The day might be after that early frost
Of May which harms many of the blossoms.
No, we are not sure anywhere,
The countdown is without publication,
The opulence of summer does not help.
We are left only with theory. Note
That the radiate apple petals did not
Need even a fragile wind to fall.

What is less glory than life itself?
A man dying not knowing when,
That's what, he of godly
Birth pommelling for lack of air,
Helpless obeisance to finality.
The end should be set out brutally
In health, for lovers, both at once,
Without penalty for being.
Should it not, should it not?

It's no use. We can't compete, not
With a short-lived gooseberry, not with C-natural.
A maelstrom of petals, a flash of water,
Nature's beyond us—what quality we have
Is cogitation. The advantage is nature's.
We are vanity, neither jubilant
Dolphin, impervious duck. We have
What the Preacher says we have.

Sleep done, sunstruck
We wake to morning,
Rattle in the kitchen,
Stalling, yawn,
Stretch out of yesterday,
Have mortality.

☙

An ordering of accurate words
    Will do.

To Scriabin, F$^{\#}$
At 383 vibrations a second
Was bright blue, to Rimbaud, each
Vowel was a different colour—sensation
Held to true account, thisness
Exacted, meaning in exactness transcendent,
Each to each, as time, as breathing
Is, as tide suggests the moon,
As stone, Druids' haulings, Stephen
Martyred, though stone is stone, indurate,
Impassive, beyond harmonics and itself.
Double allocation, language
In poetry! depth and degree of breath
The meaning, let metrics clash as they will,
The rhythm right, the meaning the hearing,
Rough or smooth, all is the hearing.
What is meant, said; how,
The delight—not self-conscious nor sloven,
Not constrained, the tempering power

The heart; emotion alert for the vowel,
The consonant's unobtrusive constancy.
Movement, resonance, true silence!
English, grand unparalleled music!

Image against image, spilled
Quicksilver! that's one way,
Velasquez, Pound, Klee;
Narrative breathless, another, a going
Richness: Chopin, El Greco, Liszt;
The third as music (almost solely—
Syntax to the devil if need be):
Stevens, Kandinsky—all those
Who hate tin ears. *Ut doceat,*
Moveat, delectet, Shakespeare
Incomparable! So it exists this poetry.

⚜

Safe at home, her beside me! Hours
Still to go until she is back, music
On the stereo, in the middle of the Mozart
The bellow of the cow not ours a half mile off
Full of milk and Uranus beaming facing
The rocketed telescope amid the unblinking stars.

Committees re-position commas. I wish
She was home, the doors unlocked all over the house.
It's winter. My heart aches—the logs burning,
Snow falling, happiness possible,
Salt oceans tumbling and so on . . .

It is the gayety she has, going off,
Her umbrella aslant, loving the thunder,
An unduckable challenge to calamities
Should they exist. She knows, of course
She knows, how sorrow when least wanted
Enters in, how shoes, eventually,
Get soaked, as a child she knew: worse
Than indifference, love that demeans.
Everyone knows sorrows. A birthright.
She angles her umbrella sheltering
The world, wears her best shoes
In the rain—the ones in two colours,
Grey and green brought all
The way from Venice, the shop at the next
Corner just up from the Rialto bridge
Where Antonio did not know why
He was so sad. She does.
She has sordid sorrows cornered.

      O I shall prove that the hatred
      In the Middle East is curable.
      I have turned on the footpath lantern
      That works with the lamp on the verandah.
      The three steps up
      To the walk are well lighted.
      It was to the postoffice she went.
      To mail a birthday card.
      The power of love is more
      Than theory, she is back on the verandah.
      We watch the blue-footed
      Booby on TV
      Dance. The bird reminds me
      Of Joplin's piano-jig.

Have you seen the blue-footed booby dance—
One foot, the other, Joplin's ragtime rocked?
You must see that before you leave for heaven.
And the penguin in white-tie slide on his bottom
Ice down to the slippery sea for fish?
That too is worth interrupting
Adding and subtracting for. The prospect alone
Cancels any impulse to get it over with. Watching
The hummingbird confront a tipped scarlet
Trumpet will do this, a skyscraper
Going up, oil-patches watched.

> Notice that the scales of drying fish
> Wet in the sun, are iridescent;
>
> That lack of stones deepens water.
> The grain of wood sustains study.
>
> It was as if I tasted cinnamon examining
> The nature of mahogany.
>
> Snow is a fit subject for logic.
> The look of an equation is sufficient.
>
> One could do worse than propound
> The shaded moss-side of a boulder.
>
> Within a building a light shines,
> They work at night. No one talks.

❦

Hamlet's shadows, Akhmatova's ghosts,
Old sorrows, what are old sorrows to me?
The arras is drawn, St. Petersburg survives.
What phantoms matter? Cassandra's loves,
Richard's princes in the Tower, the staircase
Silent? Niobe's weeping headstones,
Eurydice, Orpheus' broken lute? All
The ceaseless sorrows. Endurance only matters,
Mephistopheles' shrug and the plunge where
The last ruby sinks in the pond mossy
With forgetfulness. Let us sit and
Contemplate while horses' hoofs pound
Riderless across apocalyptic skies.
O vasty emptiness, sorrows of Lebanon,
Candelabra gutter above cloth of shrouds!

❧

Fugue

Counterpart to all we had seen:
Lemon sole at the Mitre
In Oxford, going from country to country: a fifth,
Sixth, immortality come on,

Remembered men's work or anonymous.
I learned what I had guessed:
Love matters; food is necessary—
I eat the means and seek ends.

Simple enough to what only matters: Greek
Ictinus building proportion,
Marble Parthenon, Venus standing
On her birthday cockleshell,

Anonymous "Sumer is icumen in,"
VINCENT in big letters—
Whatever's given in adversity: Pope's
Disfigurement, Quasimodo;

Schumann who couldn't compose, Clara who couldn't
Compose, each within earshot,
Who loved each other; Monet and his painted
Boat secure among the water's

Lilies where the reflected willows weep.
The richness of the world!
The Lord's prayer engraved on the head of a pin
As if heaven would come!

The achievement found at the end of things:
The lessening of an ability to know.
Mist on a clear night of the moon,
Truth of a change troubling exactness
That is itself. World and fatal
Heaven, the paradox . . .

I am next to midnight,
Almost I hear the bell toll—
Assurance I could do without.
I have no answer, faith the warrant
Of intransigence I would not leave.
Sensation claims me, I leave my love.

❧

Index

Also by Ralph Gustafson

Poetry

The Golden Chalice   1935
Alfred the Great   1937
Epithalamium in Time of War   1941
Lyrics Unromantic   1942
Flight into Darkness   1944
Rivers among Rocks   1960
Rocky Mountain Poems   1960
Sift in an Hourglass   1966
Ixion's Wheel   1969
Selected Poems   1972
Theme & Variations for Sounding Brass   1972
Fire on Stone   1974
Corners in the Glass   1977
Soviet Poems   1978
Sequences   1979
Landscape with Rain   1980
Conflicts of Spring   1981
Gradations of Grandeur   1982
The Moment Is All: Selected Poems 1944-83
Solidarnośč: Prelude   1983
At the Ocean's Verge   1984
Directives of Autumn   1984
Impromptus   1984
Twelve Landscapes   1985
Manipulations on Greek Themes   1987
Winter Prophecies   1987
The Celestial Corkscrew   1989
Shadows in the Grass   1991
Configurations at Midnight   1992
Tracks in the Snow   1994

Short Stories

The Brazen Tower   1974
The Vivid Air   1980

Essays

Plummets & Other Partialities   1987

Letters

A Literary Friendship:
The Correspondence of Ralph Gustafson and W. W. E. Ross   1984

Anthologies (as editor)

Pelican Anthology of Canadian Poetry   1942
A Little Anthology of Canadian Poets   1943
Canadian Accent   1944
The Penguin Book of Canadian Verse   1958, 1967, 1975, 1984